Garter Snakes

Garter Snakes

Their Natural History and Care in Captivity

ROGER SWEENEY

BLANDFORD

Blandford
An imprint of Cassell,
Villiers House, 41–47 Strand, London WC2N 5JE

First published in the UK 1992

Distributed in the United States by
Sterling Publishing Co., Inc.
387 Park Avenue South, New York,
N.Y. 10016–8810

Distributed in Australia by
Capricorn Link (Australia) Pty Ltd.
P.O. Box 665, Lane Cove, NSW 2066

**British Library Cataloguing in Publication
Data**
Sweeney, Roger
  Garter snakes.
  1. Snakes
  I. Title
  597.96

ISBN 0 7137 2271 1

Phototypeset by Intype, London
Printed and bound in Great Britain by
Biddles Ltd., Guildford and King's Lynn

Contents

Acknowledgements

In writing this book it is necessary to thank many people, but principally Keith Brown and Isolde Mc-George for their help, advice and discussion relating to all matters herpetological over the past years and for their critical proof reading of the text; the herpetological staff at the British Museum (Natural History) for their assistance with taxonomy and tracing relevant information; Barbara Graham for her line drawings to help illustrate the text; and finally David Harvey for also assisting in the obtaining of relevant information and valuable advice as to the production of this book.

Photographic Credits

Aquila Photographic Agency: photographs 1 and 2 in the colour section.

Chris Mattison: photographs 3, 5, 6, 7, 8, 9 and 10 in the colour section. Photographs 8 and 9 are also used on the jacket.

Roger Sweeney: photograph 4 in the colour section.

Editorial Note

Metric Conversions

Throughout this book all measurements of temperature and length are given as metric.

Those readers who are more familiar with the Fahrenheit thermometer or the Imperial System of measurement might find the following formulae and conversion tables useful.

Temperature

To convert °C to °F:

$\times 9 \div 5 + 32$

Length

To convert cm to in:

$\div 2.54$

°C		°F	cm		in.
10	=	50	1	=	0.39
15	=	59	10	=	3.94
20	=	68	20	=	7.87
25	=	77	30	=	11.81
30	=	86	40	=	15.75
35	=	95	50	=	19.66
40	=	104	60	=	23.62
45	=	113	100 (1m)	=	39.37 (3.3ft)
50	=	122	200 (2m)	=	78.74 (6.6ft)
			400 (4m)	=	157.48 (13.1ft)

Distance

To convert km to miles:

$\times 0.62$

km	miles
1 =	0.62

Preface

Snakes of the genus *Thamnophis* are found right across the United States of America from Canada in the north reaching down to South and Central American countries such as Honduras, Costa Rica and Nicaragua. As with most groups of animals their taxonomy is continually under review and although there are widely accepted standards for the classifying of species occurring mainly in the United States the taxonomy of species from Central America and particularly Mexico is subject to much confusion and most works on this area differ markedly in their findings.

This book has been written primarily as a guide for people contemplating keeping Garter Snakes as pets, but aims also to provide additional information on the natural history of these and other snakes to promote better understanding of the needs of captive snakes in general. As such it contents itself with describing mainly all the species that are ever likely to be available.

The taxonomy used in this book is based on literature cited in the Bibliography and other available sources principally the British Museum (Natural History) to which I am grateful. As far as I am aware it is accurate at the time of writing although I accept responsibility for any mistakes and would welcome correspondence with anyone working in the taxonomy of reptiles in this region.

Roger Sweeney
June 1990

Introduction

The idea of keeping snakes as 'pets' is not a new one; indeed, it has been around for many generations. There has always been a fascination with snakes in many people that equals the fear expressed by others. Since tales began about the serpent in the Garden of Eden, who enticed Eve to take the forbidden fruit, there has been a strong mythology surrounding snakes and to a lesser extent other reptiles. However, while generally viewed by many with fear and often associated with visions of evil and death, snakes have not always had a completely bad press, for when the Roman Empire extended across Europe they carried with them the Aesculapian snake which they viewed as a symbol of health and fitness. This was treated with respect and tolerance when encountered in the wild and kept with the most dedicated care in the cities. The fear of snakes which is widespread in people the world over is not instinctive but rather taught very early in life either by peers or, most commonly in the West, by the media.

The main fear surrounding snakes has developed quite understandably from the fact that there are many venomous species. In areas where there are high densities of venomous snakes, and particularly in countries which have less well developed medical services, such as India and many parts of Africa, fatalities resulting from snake bites do take place regularly. It is interesting, however, to note that people living in such areas and encountering snakes, many of them highly venomous, have less of an instinctive fear of them but rather treat them with the respect they deserve. Venomous snakes which are found in the vicinity of villages are normally quickly dispatched, but this treatment is not extended to the harmless species, which are normally tolerated with little interference. By comparison people from Western countries often fear all species of snake, even in countries which do not have venomous species.

Attitudes towards snakes are now rapidly changing. As the level of public awareness increases about the plight of the many endangered plants and animals around the world facing extinction, so also grows the level of interest and tolerance, towards the less under-stood and less well-known animals, including snakes, which have until now been neglected. The era of the television nature documentary programme has awakened whole new areas of public interest in the countryside and the animals that inhabit it, and this has certainly been to the benefit of snakes which in the past have suffered more than most from inaccuracy and folk lore.

In writing this book I hope that interest in Garter Snakes and the resulting larger-scale appearance of them in the pet trade can be matched by improving standards of captive care and understanding. The popularity of snakes such as Garter Snakes, while providing the oppor-tunity for much wider interest and understanding of snakes in general, which must be to the advantage of all future herptile conservation projects, may in itself prove problematic to those species most desirable as captive pets. The pet trade cannot just keep taking animals from the wild to supply demand. If captive populations are to grow, it must be as a result of increased breeding from snakes already widely kept in captivity. Many of the *Thamnophis* species are among the easiest of snakes to keep and breed, so they should show the way in this respect, and taking them from the wild should become unnecessary once captive breeding starts to match demand. Many species face a harsh future in the wild even before their populations are harvested for the pet trade, and it may very soon be that the populations already present in captivity will become the only real hope for the survival of many species.

Garter Snakes, then, have an important future to play in conservation in a number of ways. They are perfect ambassadors in overcoming people's prejudice against snakes; they are already widely bred but can prove an ideal model for the development of better husbandry techniques; and they may well serve as the training ground for new generations of herpetologists who may graduate from keeping them to joining in with the work of the many herpetological societies. These societies not only promote new ideas in snake husbandry but often also involve themselves in conservation projects locally and nationally. The addresses of many of these societies are listed on page 124 of this book, and it is hoped that a good proportion of the people interested in keeping snakes will involve themselves in the work of these groups.

Part One

Natural History

Anatomy

The anatomy of snakes is among the most specialized and certainly among the most interesting of any group of animals alive today. The body structure, and particularly the absence of arms and legs, has led to the development of a series of unique styles of movement, hunting, feeding, courtship and breeding that are different from those of any other group of living animals. The snake's diet of whole animals has not only led to the development of a highly specialized digestive system that allows for the swallowing of prey items that would at first appear greatly oversized for the snake to manage, but also allows for prey which has a covering of particularly thick or coarse hair and skin to be digested – in many other animals the digestion of such food items would prove far too difficult. Most species of snake in the world today are terrestrial in their lifestyle; some, however, are arboreal and as such tend to be very long and slender in build, often being found in high trees or bushes; a few are burrowing species and live mainly underground, rarely ever seen on the surface. *Thamnophis* species of snakes are predominantly terrestrial, although with their slender build and agile abilities they can often be observed climbing or swimming across the wide variety of differing habitats in which they occur throughout America.

Skeleton

The skull of a snake is of a highly manoeuvrable but also quite delicate design and it is not uncommon to find captive snakes which have dislocated or broken jaws. This delicacy of skull design stems from the jaw bones being highly manoeuvrable in their sockets on top of each other in order that particularly large and wide items of prey can be swallowed whole without the need for reduction to a more manageable size by chewing. The jaws' high level of manoeuvrability allows them to move independently of each other as a further aid to swallowing difficult prey items, allowing one side of the jaw at a time to push the prey down the throat while the other side holds it (as it may well still be alive). Working like

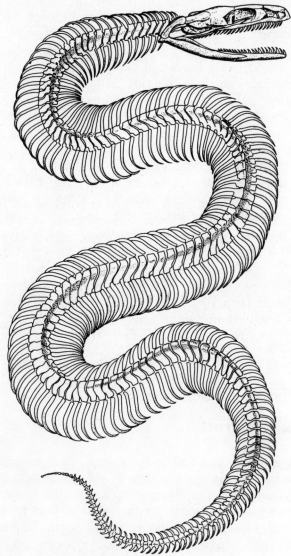

Fig. 1. Diagram of snake's skeleton.

this, both sides of the jaw can be used alternately to help work the prey down the throat. Both the upper and lower jaws have rows of recurved teeth that are used to hold prey securely once it has been captured and then help to push it down the throat as it is being swallowed. The teeth of all snakes fall out and are replaced periodically during their lifetime; teeth can sometimes be found in the faeces, having passed through the digestive tract to be expelled with other bodily waste.

In the wide variety of differing species of snake alive in the world today there can be anything from 80 to 300 vertebrae making up the spine. All but the first two of these bear paired ribs which provide the main structure of the snake's body. These vertebrae and ribs are also highly manoeuvrable, the ribs extending around to the ventral scales where they are joined across the belly by a long series of strong muscles. These muscles, as well as being fixed against the ribs, are fixed against the ventral epidermal surface and provide the means by which the snake moves along using the different movements described on pages 23–7. There are, of course, no limbs present in any living snakes and the small external spurs that can be seen in many species of larger Pythons and Boas on either side of the vent are completely lacking in *Thamnophis* species. This body structure in snakes is not only highly manoeuvrable, as can often be observed by watching a large snake squeeze through what seems like the smallest of holes, but is also very resistant to damage, and in all but the most extreme cases of accidental crushing a snake can usually survive with little apparent harm being inflicted upon the skeleton.

Digestive Tract

When a snake is swallowing a large item of prey the mouth can be opened extremely wide and the teeth are used to push the prey back into the mouth. The tongue, which is normally very predominant in the mouth, is during swallowing withdrawn into a sheath. The tubular glottis, also prominent in the mouth, being positioned behind the tongue and providing the main airway to the lungs, is manoeuvrable and during swallowing can at times be extended to the side for inspiration (breathing in). This prominent size of the glottis is also responsible for the familiar hissing sound that is associated with snakes.

The oesophagus in snakes is thinly walled and highly expandable; this is essential given the size and shape of prey that is likely to be consumed. The oesophagus leads directly into the thicker-walled but equally expandable, spindle-shaped stomach where the main digestion and breakdown of food occur. Once the prey has been broken

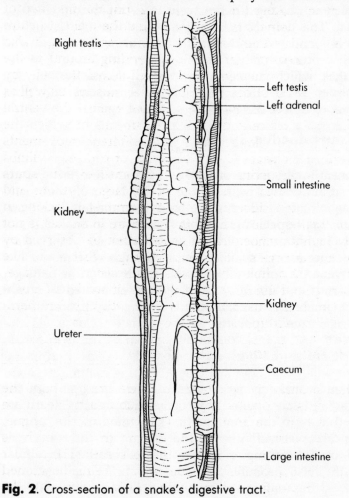

Right testis

Left testis

Left adrenal

Small intestine

Kidney

Kidney

Ureter

Caecum

Large intestine

Fig. 2. Cross-section of a snake's digestive tract.

down into a suitable state here, it can pass through the small intestine which consists of several small transverse loops and is responsible for the absorption into the bloodstream of the most usable products from the food. The large intestine that follows consists of a large, wide tube whose primary function is the absorption of liquids into the bloodstream. Fig. 2 shows a cross-section of a snake's digestive tract.

The liver in snakes is extremely large in relation to their body size and may consist of three to four separate lobes. Their other noticeable feature is the cloaca glands, which can be used defensively to excrete a foul-smelling fluid. This defence is frequently employed by *Thamnophis* species and will undoubtedly be known to anyone who has captured or handled any recently caught water snakes which all seem to defend themselves in this manner. Most of the other body organs vary little from those of other reptiles.

Reproductive System

In nearly all species of snakes the right and left gonads lie at different levels of the body, the right normally being situated higher in the body than the left. The ovaries of the female can and often do overlap on occasions, but this is not true of the testes of the male. In *Thamnophis* species the right testis of the male commonly lies between the 86th and 94th scale and the left one between the 96th and 103rd scale. They are elongated in shape and are of light colouration. During copulation sperm travels from the testes to the female's cloaca via the male's sex organs, commonly known as the hemipenes; these are paired organs that normally lie inverted in the male's tail just below the cloaca. During mating these are everted ready for use by muscular tension, and both the right and left organs may be used by the male snake alternately in one mating. In *Thamnophis* species mating can take place in autumn; the sperm from such matings is stored over winter for use the following spring if no sperm becomes available from later spring matings. Any later spring mating will stimulate follicle growth and lead

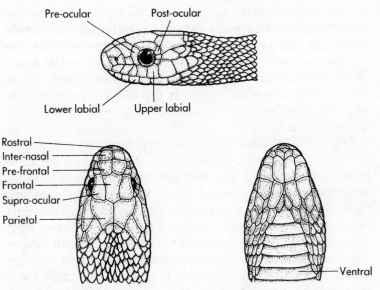

Fig. 3. The head scales of *Thamnophis* snakes.

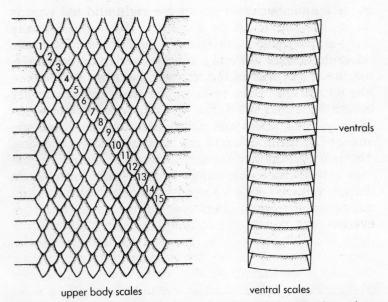

upper body scales   ventral scales

Fig. 4. Ventral and upper body scales. The numbering shows how the scale rows are counted.

to the degeneration of sperm stored over winter, but if no spring mating takes place production of young can be managed from the stored sperm. *Thamnophis* species are viviparous and the young develop inside the female's body until they are born live in membrane sacs and are fully independent as soon as they release themselves from these coverings.

Scales and Skin

The skin of a snake is rather elastic in nature, so permitting the flexibility needed when swallowing large items of prey. This skin is normally not visible to the eye as it is covered, over the length of the snake's body, by overlapping scales. However, during the swallowing of food the skin can become stretched, particularly around the area of the upper neck where the circumference of the snake's body is at its narrowest, and in such areas the skin can clearly be seen in the spaces between the stretched scales. The scales of a snake can be smooth or rough. All *Thamnophis* species have keeled scales. The exact number of scale rows over the body, the number of ventral scales and the number and make-up of scales around the head of a snake are all important in the identification of differing species within a genus. The names of the different scales that might be mentioned in the text of this book are given in Figs. 3 and 4. Contrary to old-fashioned belief, the skin of a snake is not wet or slippery. The scales are made of keratin, the same substance of which human finger nails are made, and indeed the feeling is rather similar. The scales are never shed but instead the entire outer layer of skin covering the snake is shed, leaving a perfect inside-out replica of the owner on the ground behind it.

Sloughing

Shedding of the old skin, commonly known as sloughing (see Fig. 5), is carried out periodically by all living species of snake to enable them to grow and live normally. The time periods between sloughs can vary greatly depending on the age and maturity of the snake. Young snakes which are growing rapidly may slough every four to five weeks in order that the skin keeps pace with the rapid growth of the body, while a fully grown, mature snake may need to slough only a couple of times a year. Successful sloughing is important to wild snakes as any bad sloughs which leave some of the skin still attached to the body can dramatically impair important hunting senses. The eyesight particularly can suffer as the eye lenses are often one of the main trouble spots of sloughing: the outer third eye lens, which is meant to be renewed with every cast, can fail to come off, and often snakes in captivity can be observed with up to three or even more old eye lenses built up on top of the eye from previous unsuccessful sloughings.

The main signs that the snake will soon be ready to slough are general irritability in behaviour, a lack of

Fig. 5. A snake sloughing its skin.

appetite immediately before sloughing and a general dulling of the body colouration. This dulling of the skin colour and subsequent clouding of the eyes, which become milky in appearance about three or four days before sloughing, is caused by fluid secreted from the exuvial glands which help loosen the old skin away from the body prior to a slough taking place. The eyes will later clear at least a day before the actual slough occurs.

The act of sloughing begins with the snake loosening the skin around the lips by rubbing the sides of the mouth against a convenient rock or similar rough surface. The skin over the top of the head is then rubbed back with particular care that the outer eye lens is also removed for the reasons given on page 20. The skin around the lower surface of the mouth is then peeled back with more ease as the snake simply crawls forward and in effect out of the old skin. Provided that the skin around the top of the head has been rolled back without any noticeable tearing or damage, the whole of the skin can then come off in one long undamaged inside-out strip, which will leave a perfect inside-out replica of the skin minus, of course, the colour of the scales. Such complete skins can later prove valuable in education purposes and in helping people to overcome fear of snakes. Note, however, that scale counts should not be taken from old skins as these are notoriously inaccurate; scale counts should always be taken from living snakes only.

Occasionally in the wild certain snakes will not shed perfectly, either because of a scar or similar injury that stops the skin coming off in one piece, or as a result of general poor health or dehydration. Even so, in these rare examples such snakes generally manage with a little effort to remove all the remaining skin with considerably more ease than many lazy captive specimens. The latter seem not to bother much of the time; but their wild brothers and sisters have the encouragement of wishing to avoid falling easy prey to one of the Garter Snake's many predators.

Movement

The snake's unusual structure, as described and illustrated in the section on anatomy, leads it to employ more than one unusual method of locomotion. When they are viewed from a distance, snakes seem to glide along the surface of the ground with no apparent effort. Even when they are observed more closely in a vivarium, little can be seen of the effort they displace during movement. In familiarizing a person with snakes for the first time, often the cause of greatest interest is allowing a snake to crawl over the subject's hands and arms in order that he or she can feel the snake's progression against the skin. Perhaps the most common myth regarding snake motion is the speed at which they can travel. There are many old stories of people being chased by snakes when in truth even the fastest can reach a maximum speed of only about 6½ km per hour. Such stories normally result from the exaggeration of incidences when a snake was probably discovered in a confined area such as a shed or outhouse. In such circumstances, with no obvious means of escape, the snake will usually stand its ground and attack any movement towards it, but this is far from the exaggerated stories of snakes chasing men across open ground at lightning speed.

The differing 'crawling' actions of snake species are defined differently by various herpetologists but the movements of Garter Snakes can best be explained by splitting the locomotion into three basic types.

The caterpillar-type motion (see Fig. 6) is that which can be felt when resting a snake across the palm of the hand and letting it crawl over it. This motion is the means by which a snake can move forward in what seems like a completely straight line with no apparent effort visible from above. Early explanations of this movement varied from the snake 'walking on its ribs' to 'lifting its under body in a series of waves to push itself across

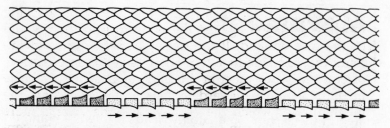

Fig. 6. Diagram showing the different movements of the snake's ventral scales during the caterpillar-type motion.

the ground', though in fact neither of these is true. The movement is actually created by inter-action between the ventral skin and the muscles connecting the ribs to the skin: a section of skin is drawn forward into a bunched state, then pushed down against the ground substrate. The body then moves forward, pulled by the appropriate muscles, until the muscles and skin are back in the normal alignment, and the movement begins again. This process is repeated along the entire length of the body, giving the snake its apparent ease of movement. This form of motion is at its most apparent when the snake is climbing or when only limited areas of its body can be pushed against a surface, such as when it is crossing branches or moving across a human hand.

The second type of motion, snaking, or the horizontal undulatory motion, as it is sometimes called (see Fig. 7), is the most common one used by Garter Snakes, but it is also probably the hardest initially to understand. The snake moves across the ground in a series of 'S'-like curves with the rear parts of the body following the exact pattern on the ground of the parts nearer the head, leaving a near-perfect line behind the snake. Such motion is a considerable advancement on the caterpillar-type and can be used with much greater speed. But it is difficult for us to grasp how the effort put into this side-to-side, curving motion is transformed into forward motion in such a controlled manner. An understanding can be gained by watching the snake swim by using practically the same motion. In swimming the side-to-side movement is much more vivid and less controlled in its appearance, probably as a result of the water creating much less friction against the body to grip than would be the case on land. It can clearly be seen during swimming that the side-to-side motion uses the outer surface of each curve to push at an angle against the available medium to force forward motion. On land, where the medium over which the snake is moving affords more grip, this motion can still be used but with greater control, giving the movement a much more elegant and effortless appearance than the act of swimming, although in both instances practically the same technique is used.

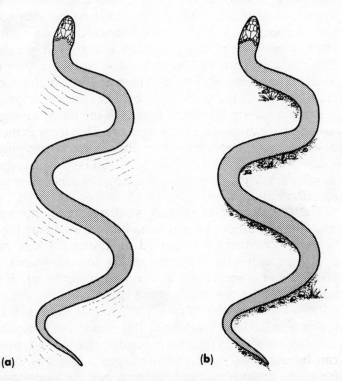

(a)   (b)

Fig. 7. Diagrams comparing the snaking motion **(a)** in water against **(b)** on land. Although the same movement is used in both cases, in water the motion is very wild and un-uniform as the medium gives little resistance against the body. On land, however, the greater friction allows the snake to use the same motion but in a more uniform fashion, leaving a perfect single trail behind it.

The third method of motion used by Garter Snakes is commonly known as the concertina-type, (see Fig. 8) named after the musical instrument. The concertina instrument opens and then draws itself together in order to supply air for sound; in the concertina motion the snake extends its head and foremost sections of its body forward and then, having secured these against the ground, will pull the remainder of its body forward in a series of movements similar to those used by an earth-

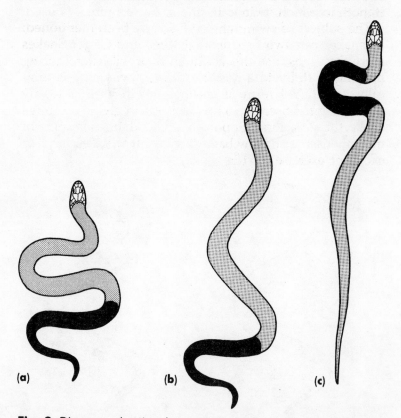

(a)   (b)   (c)

Fig. 8. Diagrams showing the concertina-type motion in a snake. In **(a)** the snake moves the front section of its body forward by pushing against the back part of the body which is 'S'ed to create maximum friction against the ground. In **(b)** the snake is shown having extended the front of the body forward. In **(c)** the snake secures the front segment of the body against the ground and uses this to pull the rear segment of body forward.

worm. This form of locomotion in Garter Snakes is perhaps the least commonly used of the three; it can at times be seen in captive snakes, usually as a result of a snake finding itself on an unfamiliar floor surface which makes the motion of snaking more difficult than would be normal.

Snake locomotion has been divided into three types to simplify their explanation, but in fact all three types are closely linked and the snake will often use a mixture of two types at the same time, depending upon the circumstances in which it finds itself.

The subject of swimming has already been mentioned: all snakes can swim surprisingly well and Garter Snakes more than most use this ability in their wild state during hunting or to avoid a possible threat. Swimming is basically a modified form of snaking but in itself is highly interesting to observe, so it is well worth giving a captive snake the occasional opportunity to exhibit this form of movement in a shallow bath of water. It will also provide excellent exercise for the snake.

Senses

The senses Garter Snakes rely on greatly for hunting and survival are sight, which in *Thamnophis* species is quite good by snake standards, 'hearing' (in snakes more correctly termed the detection of vibration from the ground) and smell and taste, which are combined in the use of the Jacobson's organ in the roof of the mouth. Many snakes, most noticeably the large Python and Boa species, are also helped in their ability to hunt by the presence of a series of small pits usually along the top edge of the upper jaw. These have a thin membrane of skin inside which makes them highly sensitive to differences in temperature and so help the snake to detect areas of heat given off by prey items. These 'heat pits' are, however, not present in any of the *Thamnophis* species, which rely mainly on the sharpness of the other senses and on their agility to hunt and capture prey.

In snakes, as in nearly all wild animals, the senses are all used in unison, so that to the casual observer it is unclear just how effective each of the individual senses is if used alone. Experiments have shown that, deprived of each of the senses one at a time, a snake can still function reasonably effectively with the use of the remaining senses, so it is clear that the balanced use of all these senses is needed to ensure that the snake is at its most competitive in the wild.

Sight

The eyesight of Garter Snakes, as in all snakes, is very poor by human or general animal standards, although because the Garter Snake is an agile diurnal hunter it probably has among the best and sharpest of all snake eyesight. Snakes generally do not have any area of the retina which is of high enough sensitivity to enable them to focus directly on an object, hence the eyes are set

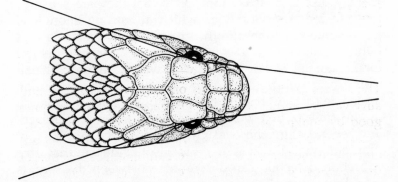

Fig. 9. The field of vision in *Thamnophis* species is more directed towards all-round and side vision than bifocal frontal vision.

fairly rigidly in the sockets and cannot move to any great extent to follow individual objects closely without some movement of the head. Snakes are also very poor at judging distances as the eyes are set on either side of the head (see Fig. 9) to allow maximum all-round vision for protection against surprise predators or to take advantage of any unexpected prey that may pass close by while they are at rest. This positioning of the eyes, however, does not allow them much overlap of vision in the front part of the snake's field of vision. This is needed to judge distances with any degree of accuracy, and it means that the snake's judgement of distance is far worse than that of other animals in which both eyes are forward-facing.

Hearing

All snakes lack external ears, and internally there is little evidence of hearing apparatus, with neither a middle ear cavity nor tympanum being present. Thus, to all intents and purposes, snakes are completely deaf in the conventional sense. Conventional hearing has to some extent been replaced by the snake taking advantage of the fact that it is extremely sensitive to vibrations passing through the substrate on which it is resting. There is even a belief by some herpetologists that snakes can also be sensitive to airborne vibrations, although this is widely disputed. It is more likely that they are sensitive only to airborne vibrations which are strong enough to send some vibration into the ground. The distance across which snakes can detect ground vibration from an object or an animal is not clear but is widely thought that it could be anything up to 5 m. Because of this it is then probable that, in many if not most cases, such a vibration is the snake's first warning that intruders are approaching, even before the eyesight has had a chance to spot the potential threat. There is also evidence that this vibration detection can differentiate between the sounds of a large animal approaching from some distance away and the more subtle sounds of a possible prey animal at a much closer distance. A combination of vibration detection and sense of smell can probably then allow the snake to start to track and hunt an item of prey even before it can be seen.

Taste and Smell

The senses of taste and smell are placed together under the same heading as nearly all snakes combine them by the use of two specially adapted sensory pits situated in the roof of the mouth and called the Jacobson's organ (see Fig. 10). In the normal behaviour of a Garter Snake the use of this organ may be observed as the snake moves around its enclosure (if captive) or especially when exploring a new and different area: the tongue will flick out and touch various obstacles in its path. Such items may be touched by the tongue several times, the tongue being withdrawn into the mouth after every taste. A more exaggerated example of this behaviour can be seen in other species such as Rattlesnakes which, when threatened, as well as responding with the usual coiling and rattling threats, also flick the tongue out and wave it in front of the head for more extended periods of time than in normal sensing behaviour. This may double as a threat gesture to an intruder as well as serving the main purpose of using the tips of the tongue to pick up air and dust particles and return them to the mouth where they can be sensed in the Jacobson's organ and so give

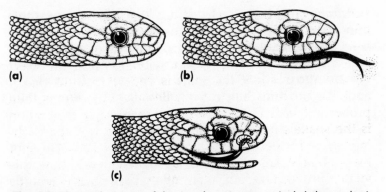

Fig. 10. The snake's use of the Jacobson's organ. In **(a)** the snake is shown in its normal position with the tongue inside the mouth. In **(b)** the tongue is shown extended, picking up air and dust particles which are then carried into the mouth as the tongue returns. In **(c)** the tips of the tongue are placed into a cavity in the roof of the mouth that houses the Jacobson's organ which analyses the particles.

the snake a better idea of the nature of the intruder facing it.

It should be noted that the Jacobson's organ is not the sole means of detection of smell by the snake as it can also be sensed through the nostrils by the more usual organ but only to a very slight extent. The Jacobson's organ is, however, unique to reptiles and perhaps, along with eyesight, is the most important sensing equipment to the long-term success and survival of the snake in nature.

Touch

The sense of touch may not at first seem to be of much relevance where snakes are concerned as they lack the limbs which in most animals carry the normal instruments of detection. Hands and feet, for example, are usually quite sensitive and are therefore associated with touching and feeling in the conventional manner. In fact the skin of most snakes is quite sensitive and can detect the slightest touch. It has already been noted that the ventral surface of the skin can sense vibrations in the substrate on which it is resting; but possibly the most important example of the snake's use of its sense of touch is in thermoregulation. In this the skin is used to detect and measure the temperature of the various areas of ground surrounding the snake as it moves from one to another, and thus helps it regulate its body temperature properly.

1. Black-necked Garter Snake, *Thamnophis cyrtopsis*, eating a frog.

2. Greater Roadrunner,
a frequent predator upon
smaller reptiles.

3. Californian King Snake, *Lampropeltis getulus californiae*, a well-known predator of smaller snake species.

4. When handled, the snake's body should be held around its mid-section with the head being supported, while at the same time it should be allowed relative freedom to move and explore.

5. Chequered Garter Snake, *Thamnophis marcianus.*

6. Western Ribbon Snake, *Thamnophis proximus*.
7. Eastern Common Garter Snake, *Thamnophis sirtalis sirtalis*.

8. Red-spotted Common Garter Snake, *Thamnophis sirtalis concinnus.*

9. Blue-striped Common Garter Snake or Florida Garter Snake,
Thamnophis sirtalis similis.

10. San Francisco Garter Snake, *Thamnophis sirtalis tetrataenia*.

Feeding

All species of snakes in the world are middle-of-the-food-chain predators. Their successful survival therefore depends on living in an environment which suits not only their own food requirements but also those of at least one species of self-sustaining prey animal. Garter Snakes, though, are rarely dependent on just one source of food but tend more to be opportunist hunters and may well feed on a wide variety of prey animals encountered over the course of a day. This is probably one of the main reasons why species of *Thamnophis* are so successful and widespread across America and why they can be found in such a diversity of natural habitats ranging from the almost entirely aquatic through to woodland and open grassland. It is also this adaptability that has enabled Garter Snakes to come to terms so well with captivity and the resulting change in diet. Anyone keeping a Garter Snake in captivity, though, even if the snake is eating well on its new diet, would be well advised to be aware of the sort of prey that the species in question might be expected to encounter in the wild. Providing your snake with the occasional different prey item that you may have found while working in the garden or visiting the countryside may well be of great assistance in helping the snake receive a balanced diet. A watchful eye should always be kept on the environment where any such food items might be collected, however, to ensure that no harmful pesticides or other chemicals have been used recently which might prove detrimental to the snake's health.

Prey

A wide selection of prey can be and is taken by Garter Snake species in the wild, ranging from aquatic invertebrates to young birds and small mammals. The main type of prey most commonly taken is likely to vary according to the habitat frequented by and the lifestyle of differing species of the *Thamnophis* group.

Mainly aquatic species (such as *Thamnophis couchi*) would be expected to feed chiefly on prey such as leeches, small freshwater fish, aquatic invertebrates, amphibian larvae, small newts and frogs; large species such as the Giant Garter Snake (*T.c. gigas*) may even take fledgling wildfowl when available.

More terrestrial species (such as *Thamnophis elegans*) make up the largest group of *Thamnophis* species and they may also include more terrestrial items of prey in their diet, such as earthworms, slugs, insects, small terrestrial amphibians and, more occasionally small mammals or birds, particularly if a nest of young is found.

It would be wrong, however, to follow any such guidelines too strictly when organizing the diet of a captive Garter Snake as all *Thamnophis* species are basically opportunists in their hunting and feeding habits and any of the above prey items may well be eaten by any one of the different species.

Hunting

In the majority of instances all Garter Snake species detect prey by means of sight or smell. As explained earlier, these are the most acute of the snake's senses. Hunting is normally a case of prey animals being encountered during the snake's daily movement through its territory, which most commonly takes place in the early morning, late afternoon and early evening when the temperature is warm without the strong direct heat of the mid-day sun. Snakes also bask for considerable periods of time each day; Garter Snakes frequently do this while on rocks overhanging an area of water or in plants also close to water. If prey comes within distance of the snake during such periods it will usually be pursued. To capture prey Garter Snakes mainly rely on their speed of movement and agility which result from their slim, agile body build.

Once seized the prey is overpowered and is normally

swallowed alive quite quickly. Garter Snakes do not possess any venom and often, because of its nature, do not constrict their food. If the prey animal is large it may sometimes be pushed up against a rock or similar object, with the weight of the snake's body holding it still while the jaws are unhinged ready for swallowing. This ability in the snake, together with the elasticity of the skin around the mouth, allows an extremely wide variety of prey items to be swallowed without too many problems. When the jaw is unhinged the sharp, backward-pointing teeth of the snake are used to work the prey down into the throat whence the strong, constricting muscle rings of the oesophagus slowly work it along to the stomach by a series of wave-like motions. The prey, if not already dead, succumbs quickly as it is swallowed.

While they feed principally on live food, there are also some reports of wild Garter Snakes eating already dead prey, especially fish. Although not widely observed, this behaviour probably occurs on the rare occasions when a snake comes across a dead prey item. The ease with which newly captured individuals adapt to eating slices of fish and similar food items offered also suggests that some degree of scavenger feeding takes place in the wild state.

Thermoregulation

The act of thermoregulation is, as the name suggests, simply the method by which cold-blooded animals such as snakes and lizards can and do to some degree regulate their own body temperature by moving from environmental areas of warmth to cool. This behaviour is common to nearly all reptiles apart from a few species that burrow and live almost completely underground, rarely appearing on the surface. Thermoregulation can, however, probably be most clearly seen in species of lizards such as those of the *Lacerta* and *Iguana* genera, but it can and does also occur in snakes.

Thamnophis species are small, slenderly built snakes and because of this they have a much higher skin-to-body-weight ratio compared to many larger and more stoutly built species of snake. This means that the Garter Snake can generally increase or decrease its ambient body temperature by exposure to differing external environment temperatures at a much quicker rate than a larger, heavier species such as an adult Python or Boa which have a lower skin-to-body-weight ratio. The use of thermoregulation allows snakes to become much more adaptable and to extend their natural range of distribution into temperate regions as well as harsh desert areas, both of which otherwise would seem to be uninhabitable by these reptiles.

The ambient temperature of the body is normally increased by the snake basking in direct heat from the sun. The area for such basking is usually a regular place which, ideally, is situated on a substrate that is not only in a position to catch the heat from sunlight but also helps to retain the heat, such as a flat rock. If the snake becomes too hot while basking, it will then simply move to a cooler area such as under wood cover or below ground until its ambient body temperature has had a chance to cool down sufficiently. It is known that Garter

Snakes can remain active and function at any temperature between 16 and 34°C, but with the use of thermoregulation they tend to keep their body temperature within a preferred range of between 22 and 31°C.

Over the normal course of a day a snake will start to bask in the early morning soon after the sun has risen. Such basking periods will be fairly long as the snake is warming up from the night before and the basking rock will also be cool, not having had time to warm up and retain the sun's heat. Most herpetologists who regularly

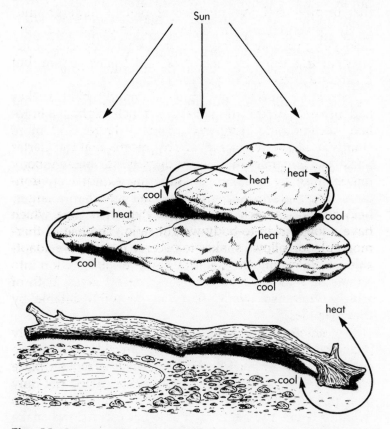

Fig. 11. Diagram showing possible patterns of thermoregulation. The arrows show how snakes can move between areas of heat and coolness in order to maintain their body temperature at the ideal level.

catch and collect wild reptiles in the field usually state that this is the best time of day to catch most species, for it is when they are most likely to make themselves visible as they seek warmth after the cool of the night. Such reptiles are generally not at this stage of the day at their most alert and agile until they have received sufficient heat. Once the ambient air temperature has warmed, the mid- to late morning is spent hunting for prey animals, up until mid-day when the heat from the sun starts to become too intense. In warm regions the middle of the day, when the temperature is at its highest, can in summer prove too hot for Garter Snakes to move about on the exposed ground, so mid-day and early afternoon are often spent in retreat under cover with only brief excursions into direct sunlight. As the temperature starts to drop slightly later in the afternoon, the snakes start to become more active, spending longer periods basking again, and hunting can often be resumed towards the end of the day. Fig. 11 shows possible patterns of thermoregulation in snakes.

The precise temperature at which Garter Snakes are most comfortable is uncertain, but it has been shown (Fitch, 1965) that when confined in a trap which is exposed to the weather but with some temperature gradient available within the trap, most Garter Snakes will use this gradient to increase their body temperature by 3–4°C – their ideal temperature, at which they seem most comfortable, appearing to be around 29–30°C.

Hibernation

Like all reptiles, snakes are cold-blooded animals, but this term might at first be misleading to anyone unfamiliar with herptiles for their blood isn't actually cold but warm as in nearly all animals. What the term 'cold-blooded' actually means is that snakes do not generate their own body heat as mammals and birds do but rather gain the heat they need from the environment around them. They can to some degree regulate their own body temperature by means of thermoregulation, as described above, and this enables them to inhabit many regions that would at first appear unsuitable from the point of view of climate. They are thus successful over a wider area of the globe than might be expected. However, for those snakes inhabiting fairly temperate regions, where thermoregulation can be used successfully for most of the year, in the winter months the extreme drop in the temperature and the corresponding reduction in the number of hours of sunlight available for basking mean that a period of hibernation is necessary if they are to survive for any length of time.

In captivity a period of cooler temperature, reduced hours of daylight and a reduced food supply are usually enough to simulate the effects of a period of hibernation on the snake's breeding cycle, but in the wild there is no doubt that a regular yearly hibernation period is essential to stimulate breeding behaviour as well as helping the snake survive the extremes of winter temperature.

In species such as the Red-sided Garter Snake (*Thamnophis sirtalis parietalis*), which can occur as far north as Canada, hibernation has to take place every year without fail. The first stimuli for the snake to begin readying itself for hibernation are likely to be the reducing hours of daylight and, perhaps more directly, the arrival of the first chilly nights of late summer. Having felt these, the snake will set out on what amounts to an annual migration, nearly always returning to the same hibernation den every year without fail unless it becomes destroyed. The distance covered by migrating snakes is uncertain but is probably up to about 3½ km over the course of several days. The reason for such site loyalty is not really known or understood, but the annual congregation of hundreds of individuals in one place during the autumn and spring has obvious important implications for the success of reproduction of the species.

On arriving at the hibernation dens, some mating does occur – possibly as a safe-guard should successful mating fail to take place for any reason in the spring after emergence. Snakes do not generally go into hibernation straight away but rather make use of whatever warm sunlight is available during the day and retreat into the dens at night in order to avoid freezing temperatures which would undoubtedly prove fatal to them. As the winter hardens, they enter a state of complete hibernation deep within the dens where the temperature never drops below 3–4°C, even in the depths of winter. Because they are cold-blooded their metabolic rate is slowed to such an extent at these low temperatures that they can comfortably remain dormant for anything up to sixteen weeks without any serious loss of body weight or condition. This is, of course, dependent on their having had a reasonable chance to build up suitable fat deposits by heavy feeding during the previous late summer leading up to the period of hibernation.

Snakes' emergence from hibernation does not happen quickly when spring arrives. Even with the beginning of a series of warm days, a week or two will pass before the temperature inside the dens warms up enough to allow the snakes to become active again. Even when they are awake they will take time to become fully active, and to begin with content themselves with brief excursions to the entrance of the den to bask during the middle of the day, returning inside before nightfall when the temperature again drops. This could well prove to be an instinctive safeguard as premature dispersal from the den sites in spring might leave the newly emerged snakes exposed to late hard frosts which they would not be able to withstand, with disastrous results for the success of the species. Male snakes tend to become fully active sooner than females, probably as a reproductive trigger, so that as the females emerge and are ready to depart from the dens there are large numbers of sexually active males ready for mating which should ensure a high level of successful pregnancies among the females.

This adaptive behaviour of Garter Snakes has, then, proved highly important, not only providing a means of surviving harsh winter conditions but also leading to a high level of reproductive success. The one major drawback of the system is the exposed nature of the population soon after their emergence in spring. Such a high number in one area of individuals which are not yet fully active can lead to problems from natural predation and overexploitation from reptile collectors. It must be remembered that the snakes present at the den represent the populations for quite a large surrounding area, so to overcollect would lead to an imbalancing of the natural population of that extensive area. Such spring collecting is also responsible for the high level of imbalance between males and females in captivity, for it is almost certainly the male snakes which are most abundant at this time of year as they are preparing themselves for the females' emergence.

Defensive Behaviour

In terms of their behaviour snakes are fairly primitive animals, showing little sign of any conventional intelligence but rather for the most part relying primarily on instinct. This instinctive behaviour controls everything the snake does from hunting through to breeding, and although such behaviour is at first sight very subtle, with careful observation a more detailed picture of its patterns can be gained by the keeper which may not only lead to a better understanding of the snake but also help the keeper to make changes to the snake's husbandry, such as variations in vivarium temperature or furnishing. The behaviour of Garter Snakes while hunting or breeding is covered elsewhere in this book, but perhaps the most marked and easily observed behaviour is that shown by the snake when it feels threatened.

Defensive behaviour in Garter Snakes can be clearly seen in nearly all recently caught specimens. When approached they will usually lift the upper part of the body into a coil in readiness for a possible strike on an oncoming aggressor. The head is held high and the tongue flicks out for longer than usual periods in order to try to sense the nature of the apparent threat. The tail of the snake will shake quickly and loudly, possibly to give the impression that it is a species of Rattlesnake with which Garter Snakes often share their territory. The large nature of the snake's tubular glottis gives rise to the commonly encountered hissing sound that occurs in nearly all species of snakes; this slowly increases and becomes louder to threaten an oncoming attacker. If the threat continues to approach and the snake has no obvious route of escape, it may well strike. As Garter Snakes have no form of venom and do not have a particularly strong bite, they will frequently feign a strike, stopping short of the object or striking with the mouth closed in order to prevent injury to the jaw.

If all this fails to prevent the snake from being seized by the aggressor, it has one last line of defence: the secession from the cloaca of a foul-smelling liquid which will often put off a predator intending to eat the snake and will certainly make handling the snake in captivity unpleasant. Fortunately this last trait is usually quickly lost in captivity once the snake becomes used to being handled and loses most of its fear of humans.

Predators

Although Garter Snakes, and indeed all living species of snakes, are predators, feeding on a wide diversity of smaller prey animals, they are also themselves the subject of predation by other larger predators. Garter Snakes' predators can roughly be divided into four main groups: reptiles, birds, wild mammals and domestic animals. A fifth area of predation has come much more into the public eye over the course of the last ten to fifteen years: the collection of Garter Snakes for the pet trade. On the whole such collecting, as long as it is regulated, is of little long-term consequence to the more commonly encountered species. It is worth repeating, however, that at certain times of the year, particularly just before the snakes enter and just after they leave the hibernation dens, when they are congregated and most easy to catch, the sex ratios from such catches are likely to be highly unbalanced, the males normally outnumbering the females several times. Such unbalanced shipments of snakes into captivity can upset breeding patterns in the wild and lead to an excess of unwanted males in captivity, so severely limiting the success of breeding attempts among captive snakes. It also goes without saying that collection of species or sub-species which have restricted ranges, such as the San Francisco Garter Snake (*Thamnophis sirtalis tetrataenia*), can dramatically affect the viability of the wild population's future; in fact most such rarer sub-species are legally protected from generalized collecting.

Reptile Predators

By far the most famous of the North American reptile predators which may feed on Garter Snakes are the many species of King Snakes. The most common species (*Lampropeltis getulus*) can be found in a wide variety of differing sub-species right across the continent. King Snakes, which usually kill their prey by constriction, can easily manage to overcome and consume snakes even of a similar width and up to two thirds of their own length. Garter Snakes, then, because of their relatively small size and light build, prove easy opportunist prey for King Snakes if they are encountered. The predominant food source for King Snakes is, however, small mammals, and although reptiles will be taken if they are found, stories of King Snakes living exclusively on other reptiles have been greatly exaggerated.

Other species of snake are also known to feed upon Garter Snakes and other small reptiles. These include the Arizona Coral Snake (*Micruroides euryxanthus*), which feeds primarily on smaller snakes; the Eastern Coral Snake (*Micrurus fulvius*), which feeds mainly on small lizards and snakes; and other medium-sized colubrid snakes, which feed mainly on small mammals but have also been known to feed on smaller reptiles if they are encountered. These include the Gopher Snake (*Pituophis melanoleucus*) and the Black Racer (*Coluber constrictor*).

On occasions some species of American lizards will capture and consume smaller types of snake, particularly juveniles. Such species of lizard include the Leopard Lizard (*Gambelia wislizenii*) and the Jungle Runner (*Ameiva ameiva*). Any such feeding behaviour by these lizards is mainly opportunist as their main diet consists of varying types of insects and also occasionally smaller lizards.

Bird Predators

Bird predation, particularly by American birds of prey, is probably the largest single source of predation among Garter Snakes, accounting for more lost snakes than any of the other three main groups of predators.

The Roadrunner is perhaps the best-known American bird predator of snakes. Even if many accounts of its exploits with larger snakes are somewhat exaggerated, smaller snakes such as Garter Snakes and lizards do undoubtedly make up quite a large segment of its food intake. The capture of such snakes and lizards is accomplished mainly by the bird's speed of movement across the ground. Once found, the prey is swiftly despatched with the aid of the bird's powerful feet and bill.

The American Kestrel and any other kestrel species found in conjunction with Garter Snakes are opportunist feeders by nature and will feed quite extensively on snakes if they are in abundance. The birds capture these snakes in true kestrel fashion, known the world over: they spend many hours hovering over an area of meadow or grassland and then swiftly swoop down to the kill once a prey item has been spotted from the air.

Various species of kite that occur in America will feed on Garter Snakes, including the Swallow-tailed, the Black-shouldered and the Mississippi Kites. These feed mainly on more arboreal species of snake, found in bushes or even in trees, as most of their time is spent in flight while hunting and they rarely perch and watch for movement on the ground which is the more normal method of detecting snakes used widely by many species of birds of prey.

Various harriers and hawks take Garter Snakes regularly if they are abundant. The harriers normally hunt by flying low across grasslands and open fields, while the hawks frequently perch and watch for movement on the ground below.

Wild Mammal Predators

Very few mammals in the world specialize in hunting and eating snakes as their main diet. Even the famous mongoose in Africa and Asia, which is credited with being the world's most effective snake predator, does in fact live mainly on a diet that contains snakes but also lizards, insects, small mammals and occasionally young birds. Most carnivorous mammals are mainly opportunist feeders and will take snakes as food if they are easily available as part of a wide selection of prey.

The wild mink, which is common across much of the range of many Garter Snakes, is for its size perhaps the world's most formidable predator and will kill prey items often larger than itself with surprising ease. Garter Snakes, therefore, are easy pickings for such an aggressive predator and are commonly taken if and when they are discovered.

Other small American carnivores, such as skunks and opossums, will also take Garter Snakes as prey if they uncover them while scavenging. They also eat other small reptiles, such as lizards, and even larger insects.

Some of the larger species of American carnivores, like raccoons and badgers, are both known to eat snakes from time to time, although the size of Garter Snakes suggests that such larger predators are unlikely to expend too much energy trying to capture them because of the limited food potential of small snakes. Other large predators such as peccaries, coyotes and bobcats, all of which are also known occasionally to capture and consume snakes.

Domestic Animal Predators

Without doubt the greatest detrimental effect created by the introduction of a domestic animal on endemic animal populations around the world is that caused by the domestic cat. Other introduced domestic species, notably the rat and rabbit, have also inflicted damage on local ecosystems, but it is the cat in its highly effective role as a household predator that has wreaked havoc, being introduced to areas where the existing local fauna is not used to or has not been adapted to the presence of such a type of predator. Luckily the Garter Snake has not been so badly affected as it has evolved with a whole host of natural predators which have aided its adaption. The cat is, however, a very successful predator in general, being very agile, quick and light-footed, qualities which make it certainly one of the best adapted of all mammal predators of snakes. Apart from feral populations, which are not that widespread in uninhabited areas, the main cat populations are grouped around areas of human population, so they are usually unlikely to threaten the main snake populations but could be a major factor in the decline of rare sub-species that are dependent on a restricted range which is near areas of human habitation. Such snake populations are normally small by nature, and added to the problems of human interference and rapid habitat change that can take place in urban areas, the presence in large numbers of such a lethal predator as the cat can prove fatal.

There are also occasional reports of certain farm animals killing snakes. These reports commonly mention sheep, pigs, chickens and most especially horses. Such cases are rare and cannot really be termed as predation in its conventional sense, but are more likely to be the result of an instinctive fear in the animals mentioned, especially if the region in which they live has local venomous species of snake.

Reproduction

The breeding biology of wild populations of Garter Snakes is highly dependent on climatic changes which are subject to the region in which the snakes occur. *Thamnophis* species are, however, distributed so widely across North and Central America that there are considerable variations between different species and sub-species. As an example, one of the most commonly seen species, the Red-sided Garter Snake (*Thamnophis sirtalis parietalis*) will be used to describe breeding behaviour, although in other species from more tropical regions the behaviour in the winter months is likely to be less extreme and last for a much shorter time. The graphs shown on page 50 indicate the variations over a year of the average hours of daylight and average maximum temperature levels. These graphs are provided as a guide to anyone trying to recreate the natural conditions which stimulate snakes to reproduce.

Snakes by nature are solitary animals, not generally mixing or congregating for most of the year except in unusual circumstances. This would normally make breeding, and more particularly mating, a rather haphazard affair, being mainly dependent on two snakes of the opposite sex coming across each other at the right time of year. Snakes have no means of oral communication and the only senses available to help them find a suitable mate are sight and smell. The use of communal hibernation dens, as described earlier, is therefore of considerable importance if a reasonable level of successful reproduction of the species is to take place over a prolonged period of time.

Mating commonly takes place in late autumn as the snakes start to congregate before their hibernation period in the dens. The sperm from such matings is not used straight away but stored by the female over winter in case no successful mating occurs the following spring. Normally, however, the sperm from the autumn matings is allowed to degenerate once a successful mating has taken place in the spring. The process of hibernation, and in particular the lowering of the female's body temperature, leads to changes in the effectiveness of different hormones which in turn lead to the ovaries being stimulated ready for egg production in the spring.

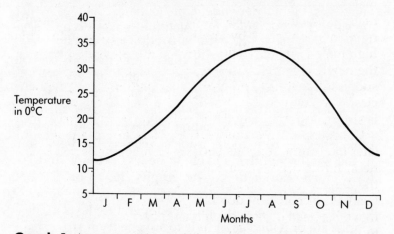

Graph 1. Average maximum daily temperature over the course of a year.

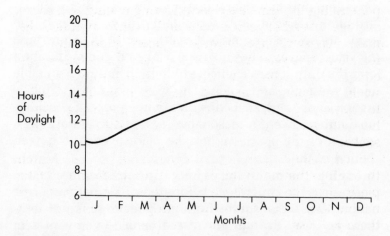

Graph 2. Average number of hours of daylight over the course of a year.

Towards the end of the hibernation period the male snakes will normally start to become active first. They usually make their way to the outside of the den to bask and regain their senses several days before the female snakes do. By the time the females start to become active and appear from the hibernation dens, nearly all the males have become sexually active and are ready for mating. As the females slowly appear they can be outnumbered by males by anything up to fifty to one. This high male-to-female ratio, added to the sluggish nature of the newly emerged females, leads to a high percentage of successful matings and a resulting high level of pregnancies. The competition between the males trying to mate is strong and naturally the strongest males are successful.

Courtship during this period is less important than in later or autumn matings because of the females' sluggishness, but it usually starts with the male snake following the female while she crawls across the floor, with his head about half-way down her body. The male will then move his head over to the female's back and start to begin to nudge it with his chin. This nudging continues as the male slowly works his way up the side of the female until the vents of both snakes are parallel. The female will then usually permit copulation to take place, with the male erecting one of his hemipenes at a time and penetrating the female's cloaca. During mating, which on average takes between fifteen and twenty minutes, the male may well use both hemipenes alternately. The female may try to move but the male's hemipenes are equipped with barbs which hold them firmly in place while copulation takes place, so that if the female tries to crawl away the male will just be dragged along behind her with no obvious discomfort being shown by either snake.

Such matings are normally observed in late March through to the beginning of May. Later matings also take place after the snakes have dispersed from the hibernation dens should individuals of opposite sex meet, but these are less frequent and probably of less importance than the matings immediately after leaving the hibernation dens.

The young which should result from such matings are always born live, normally during the months of August to September and even as late as October in the northern-most reaches of the Garter Snake's natural range. Such young are fully independent from the start as soon as they are free of the membrane skin that covers them at birth and commonly measure 13–23 cm in initial birth length. The diet of these newly born snakes consists basically of any earthworm, invertebrate or fish prey items that are small enough to be overcome and swallowed by the neonates which, apart from their size, are exact replicas of their parents. The young snakes have to feed avidly for the first few months of their lives in order to grow sufficiently and put on enough weight to be able to survive their first winter. Because of this the young are surprisingly aggressive when encountering prey and can overcome quite large prey items for their small size. If they can survive this most dangerous period of their lives, when they are extremely vulnerable to predation by other snakes as well as a whole host of other predators, they will normally go on to grow steadily in length until they become fully mature, usually after their second year.

Part Two

Captive Husbandry

Housing

When considering the appropriate container for housing a Garter Snake, the first essential is that it must be completely escape-proof. Captive snakes are notorious escape artists: the smallest gap can provide a possible exit from the enclosure. Even the presence of a shelf or ridge underneath the top of a glass tank may offer the snake a chance to manoeuvre the lid loose and so lead to an escape.

While being completely secure, the container should at the same time be well ventilated. Although Garter Snakes are well used to living next to or in water, it is a mistake to keep them in too high a level of humidity as this can lead to health problems later, particularly in the more terrestrial species.

A bathing area should always be present but, having emerged from this, the snake should be able to move to a heat spot to dry out. The size of the enclosure can vary but it should be big enough to allow separate areas of warmth and coolness, a bathing area and suitable furnishings which will allow the snake to move and behave adequately and provide differing textures to rub against which may well help it when it is sloughing. Finally, whatever type of container is used, it should be able to be heated to the snake's requirements. Provided these considerations are met, any of a wide range of differing containers can be used to house snakes adequately, the most common of which are described below.

Types of Vivarium

By far the most common means of housing captive Garter Snakes is in the combination of a glass aquarium tank with a custom-made vivarium lid (see Fig. 12). The glass tank has many points in its favour: it is easy to keep clean, it is waterproof and it offers good all-round visibility. The vivarium lid, if properly fitting, is secure and

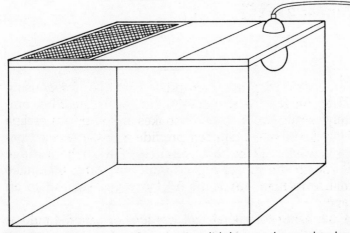

Fig. 12. A glass tank with a vivarium lid that can be used to house Garter Snakes.

allows good ventilation, easy access and has provision for lighting equipment. If the tank is seated on a poly-styrene base, heat can also be given from a source pos-itioned between this and the tank. Such vivariums are usually relatively easy to locate and purchase. Sizes of tanks and vivarium lids vary and it should not be difficult to find one of an ideal size to fit in with your existing furniture and to the amount of space you can afford to give to the enclosure. Height is also variable and can be used to great advantage when furnishing the interior for the best visual effect: vivariums can be made to look most attractive.

The second most common form of enclosure used is a wooden vivarium with overlapping sliding glass doors on the front (see Fig. 13). Ventilation is normally pro-vided via holes in the side which are usually covered by fine wire, mesh and because of the wooden construction light and heat sources can be attached directly to the interior walls or ceiling. Heating is commonly provided low down on the back wall, encased so as to prevent injury to the snake from direct contact. This encasement can then be incorporated into the general cage design not only to improve the vivarium's appearance but also to provide a heat spot for the snake's use. If it is well made,

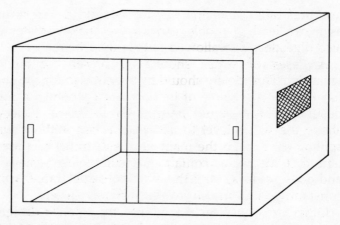

Fig. 13. A wooden vivarium with sliding glass front which can be used to house Garter Snakes.

this type of vivarium is almost completely escape-proof and a lock can be fitted to the sliding doors as an extra precaution if needed.

Variations on these two main cage designs account for nearly all available vivariums and all are generally good, although it is worth pointing out that the mainly glass types are more susceptible to extremes of weather, particularly in hot countries where care must be taken that they are not exposed to unduly large amounts of direct sunlight in warm weather which may cause excessive overheating in the snakes.

Furnishing the Vivarium

The floor of the vivarium can be covered with a number of different substrates. Newspaper can be used for the minimum of maintenance and ease of cleaning, but this is not particularly attractive to look at if the vivarium is positioned in the living room or other prominent place. A mixture of sand, peat and shingle can usually give a much better appearance and can provide a depth of substrate which can help in the hiding of objects, such as the sides of the water dish, which otherwise might spoil the appearance of the interior. Other substrates used include wood and bark shavings, but I have found these less preferable, and fine sawdust should never be used as it can lead to problems with the snake's scales and also digestion if swallowed with a food item.

An area of water should be present within the vivarium. This ideally should be big enough for the snake to immerse the whole of its body in it when in a coiled position. There should be enough clearance, however, above the water level to allow for a rise without water spilling over on to the main floor substrate. It is important that the water container is completely water-tight and does not leak, for if the main floor substrate becomes constantly damp the snake's health may suffer.

Other important inclusions into the interior design of the vivarium are a flat rock under the light bulb or other heat source to act as a basking area for the snake and suitable hiding areas where it can retreat out of the gaze of onlookers if it needs to. Such areas can be provided by pieces of bark, broken plant pots or even just dry dead leaves sprinkled over the top of the floor substrate.

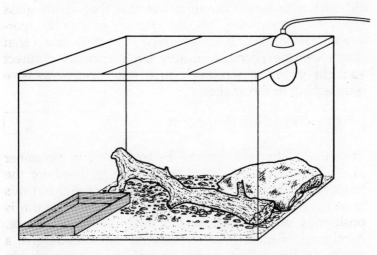

Fig. 14. A furnished snake vivarium. Important features include a water-tight water container situated away from the heating, a flat stone under the light bulb to create a heat spot and the inclusion of wood or other similar furnishings to provide a variety of textures to assist sloughing.

Branches to enable the snake to climb are also desirable, but make sure that these do not lead to the snake burning itself against the light bulb or similar heat source. The presence of both branches and stone within the vivarium is also advantageous in that they provide a diversity of textures against which the snake can rub while trying to slough its skin. Fig. 14 shows a fully furnished vivarium.

As a final point it should be remembered when building the interior of the vivarium that it must be the subject of regular cleaning and maintenance. The water should be changed at regular intervals and any uneaten food removed as soon as possible in order to prevent the presence of flies or odour. Snake excretion should also be removed as soon as it is seen, although snakes excrete far less than other animals.

Heating

There are many different types of heating equipment available which can be used to heat reptile vivariums, but when making a choice bear in mind that two main types of heat provision must be allowed for. First and most important, the ambient cage temperature must be suitable for the vivarium's inhabitants and must be maintainable through periods of extreme external weather which could otherwise adversely affect the temperature within the vivarium. Second, where possible there should be a second less powerful heat source at one end of the vivarium to provide a thermal gradient, and if there is a large flat stone under this second heat source it will act as a basking area for the snake which will increase the variant in available temperature. If there is a light bulb already present in the design of the lid, this may well be quite suitable as the second heat source. The fact that the bulb is switched off at night does not create a problem as snakes as a rule do not thermoregulate during the night.

Types of suitable equipment can vary from heat bulbs, heat cables and heat mats through to fan heaters for the largest of zoo enclosures. For the two most commonly used types of vivariums mentioned earlier, combinations of heating equipment which should be easily available and suitable are described below.

Glass Tank with Vivarium Lid

Most commercially manufactured vivarium lids to fit aquarium tanks have a hole at one end so that a light bulb can be fitted to provide light and heat. While on its own this is not really sufficient to heat the whole of the vivarium, it can provide a useful second heat source, particularly if a basking rock is provided underneath it, which will build up heat and so increase the effectiveness

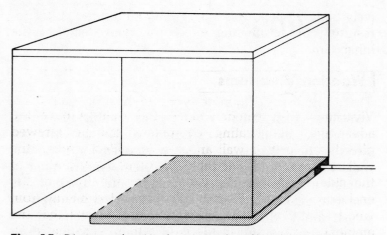

Fig. 15. Diagram showing how a carbon-fibre heat mat can be placed under a glass vivarium to provide heat.

of the source. For the main heat source I have found the easiest and most convenient equipment to be a heat mat placed under the tank (see Fig. 15), with a layer of poly-styrene under the heat mat to protect the furniture on which the tank is resting. Types of heat mat vary, but the ones I use provide about 40 watts per 30cm^2, and by the time the heat has passed through the base of the vivarium and up through the floor substrate this heat source gives a near-ideal ambient air temperature in most temperate regions where additional heat will be required. There is little or no need for a thermostat to be attached, particularly if the snake has some opportunity to regulate its own body temperature within the enclosure. How-ever, in differing climates and using differing equipment, some experimentation will probably be required before an ideal combination can be found; otherwise it may be easier just to use a more powerful heat source but always ensuring that it is attached to a suitable easily controllable thermostat. One important consideration regarding the temperature of a glass vivarium is to ensure that it is not placed in a position within the home where it will receive direct sunlight through the windows. Although natural sunlight is beneficial to all living reptiles, such cage pos-itioning during the summer months can lead to excessively high temperatures building up within the vivarium, resulting in detrimental effects or even death to the inhabitants.

Wooden Vivariums

Vivariums with wooden sides and ceilings have the advantage that heating equipment can be screwed directly on to their wall and a hole drilled through the wall so that any electric cable can be neatly taken out of the side without being visible from the front of the enclosure. Having the vivarium constructed mainly from wood also allows more insulation and means that the ambient temperature inside is of a more constant level. In such a vivarium I find that the best method of heating is to place a heat tube along the back edge of the inside and attach a thermostat which has a sensor positioned at a reasonable distance away from the heat source. Such a heat source usually provides around 40 watts per $30cm^2$ and will have to be encased in a wooden frame to ensure that the snake does not burn itself against it (see Fig. 16),

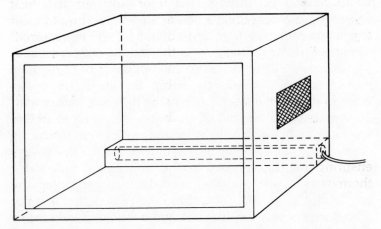

Fig. 16. Diagram showing how a wooden vivarium could be heated by including a heat tube along the bottom back edge and building a frame around it to protect the snake from direct contact.

but the encasement itself can be used to form a hot spot on which the snake can bask. If this heat source alone is not sufficient, a spotlight can be fastened to the vivarium ceiling and pointed down on to a suitable rock. Vivariums of this type may well need extra light to be provided by such spotlights or fluorescent tubes.

Feeding

As already described in Part One, the diet of most species of *Thamnophis* is based mainly on live amphibians and fish, with earthworms also being frequently taken by the more terrestrial species. Supplying snakes in captivity with live vertebrates as their main food source is not only troublesome, difficult and unnecessary but may well also lead to legal problems with animal welfare groups and similar bodies. In nearly all *Thamnophis* species the amphibian section of the diet can be replaced in captivity with no obvious nutritional detriment by increasing the amount of fish and earthworms fed, although provision should be made for dietary supplements such as multivitamin powders when necessary (see page 71).

Earthworms represent a particularly important food source for a captive snake recently acquired from the wild because as well as all the advantages to the keeper of being readily available, inexpensive and easy to collect, to the snake they are offered in very much the same form as it is used to encountering in the wild. Many of the problems of Garter Snakes not feeding when first received from the wild are due to the fact that the food being offered (normally fish) is of a type and is presented in a form not encountered by the snake before. The fish is offered dead, often cut into strips, so it has been processed in a way which is completely alien to what the snake has been used to eating in the wild. Earthworms therefore should always be offered regularly, particularly to newly acquired snakes which are only just becoming accustomed to a new type of fish in their diet. Care should always be taken, though, that the earthworms are collected from an area free of horticultural chemicals, such as weed killers or similar sprays, which could prove harmful to the snake, and as an extra precaution the earthworms should be rinsed and offered for feeding in a shallow dish to prevent them picking up undue amounts of the vivarium's floor substrate before being swallowed.

Fish, which forms the main part of the diet of most captive Garter Snakes, is on the whole a very good food source, particularly when fed in a complete form including scales and bones. For the sake of convenience it is normal to use frozen fish as this can be easily stored and defrosted when needed. As well as the types of fish available for human consumption, there are also several small varieties such as Sand Eels and Lance Fish, which can be fed whole, that are available in convenient frozen packages produced for the aquarium fish market. The use of frozen fish as the main food source does, however, have one major disadvantage. It contains an enzyme called thiaminase which digests thiamine (vitamin B1) and so leads to a deficiency of that vitamin in the snake. This problem can easily be overcome by heating the fish for about five minutes at around 80°C to destroy the enzyme. Vitamin B1 can also be given as an additive but this is not generally needed if the fish is prepared properly before being fed to the snake. If the snake is wild-caught and is reluctant to try strips of fish, try offering either Sand Eels or Lance Fish in a shallow dish of water: as well as keeping the fish fresh, the presence of water over the food will prevent flies from contaminating it. Most snakes will soon adapt to the new diet, often then taking it in preference to other food, but it is important to remember that fish should not be fed exclusively as the fat content is very high and this may lead to steatitis developing in the snake (see page 72). It must also be remembered that the fish needs to be thoroughly defrosted and brought to room temperature before being offered to the snake.

Other food sources that may be of use include pink mice, which can also be obtained in frozen form and will be taken by most of the larger terrestrial species of Garter Snake; and natural prey, such as leeches for aquatic species and slugs for terrestrial ones, which may be obtained from time to time if the opportunity arises and will be of benefit to captive snakes. Tebo Bugs and the larvae of Wax Moths, both now being widely bred and sold for the pet market, will also provide variety for Garter Snakes that will take them. Finally White Worms, which are widely available in starter culture form from tropical fish suppliers, although far too small for adult snakes to eat, may be of particular importance when trying to find large amounts of small live food for a group of newly born snakes which need to have food available in abundance so that they can find it easily and without leaving their cover.

Handling

Reptiles and amphibians in general do not make ideal pets for handling and it is best not to handle Garter Snakes too frequently, particularly if breeding is to be attempted. If breeding is not the primary object of keeping them, many Garter Snakes do adjust well to being handled and soon lose all nervousness, viewing it as a chance to explore. It should always be remembered, though, particularly if there are children present in the household, that Garter Snakes are lightly built reptiles and may suffer if handled roughly, such as by a child who tries to maintain a tight grip as the snake attempts to wander or rotate its body. Proper methods of handling and restraint are also important to enable the keeper periodically to examine the snake to check its health, to assist it in actions such as sloughing or simply to move it.

In order to let a snake become accustomed to its handler it should be held firmly around the mid-section of its body while the head is given freedom to wander and explore its surroundings. To begin with, however, if the snake is nervous, it is best to allow it to grow used to being touched by the hand inside the vivarium without actually holding it. When the hand is moved towards the snake, the flat of the palm should slowly be lowered down on top of it with fingers stretched outwards, so representing (to the snake) a broad, flat object. Once touching, the hand should be lightly rested on top of the snake while it becomes used to this. In the case of an extremely nervous snake that will not allow the hand to approach without moving away, rest a light cloth on top of the snake: once covered in this way the snake will usually settle and feel more secure, and it can then be picked up through the cloth around its mid-section and its head can be allowed to wander through the cloth where it will come into contact with the hand and accept it without taking too much notice.

When first being handled the snake should not be held inside its vivarium or other confined space, for if it panics and starts to swing its head from side to side it could damage itself against the walls or vivarium furnishings. Instead the snake should be held around its mid-section by someone sitting down so that it can explore and become used to its handler without being confined. If the snake does then start to panic, the second hand can be used gently to restrain it below the head until it can be returned to its vivarium. Any bites from Garter Snakes are unlikely even to break the skin and should be ignored, but care should be taken not to move the hand quickly if bitten or injury to the snake's jaw may result. For the most part Garter Snakes rarely bite but rather fake strikes as a threat. These are usually not followed up by an actual bite and even this behaviour is normally lost after a few days of contact and handling of a new arrival.

If the snake needs to be examined or requires assistance in sloughing, restrain it by holding the mid-section of the body with one hand while the other holds the head still by grasping it just behind the skull. If the snake is agitated at being handled for examination, it may help to keep its head dark by covering it with a cloth.

If a snake needs to be transported any distance, a wide variety of containers can be used, the most common being a cotton bag with the entrance securely sealed with an elastic band. If the bag is sealed correctly, it is probably the most escape-proof of carrying containers, but it has the disadvantage that particular care must be taken to avoid physical damage to the snake, as so soft a container affords little protection to its inhabitant. Cotton bags also give little protection against extremes in temperature. Plastic lunch boxes can easily be converted for carrying snakes with the addition of adequate ventilation. These make more sturdy containers for transportation, although care should again be taken to avoid extremes of temperature. If cold, heat or direct sunlight is likely to prove a problem during movement of the snake, the container can itself be placed inside a polystyrene box which should give adequate protection for a reasonable length of time.

Health Care

In theory snakes should be among the easiest of wild animals to keep in captivity. Their physical needs in confinement are easily met, their diet is easy to obtain, feeding does not usually need to be undertaken daily, and diseases in the wild population are few and far between. Although this is generally true, it may be something of an overstatement, particularly in the case of Garter Snakes which require slightly more attention as regards their environment and diet than other snake species. Even so, given that a snake is in good health when it is acquired, it should experience few problems other than those caused primarily by bad husbandry. Keeping a snake at the wrong temperature and/or humidity, in damp conditions and with inadequate cover in the cage can lead to skin problems, troublesome sloughing and a lack of appetite. Most of these problems can be avoided if the basic husbandry guidelines already detailed in preceding chapters are followed.

Dietary problems can occasionally arise in captive snakes, particularly if processed food is being used to feed them. Most such problems can usually be sorted out by simply avoiding certain products or by adding the correct dietary supplements to the food.

Physical injuries such as cuts, bites and burns unfortunately can occur from time to time, but can usually be treated without too much difficulty.

Parasites can be a problem in snakes. Endoparasites or internal parasites in the form of varying types of worms can be common, as can ectoparasites or external parasites such as ticks and mites. Nearly all parasites can be easily eradicated and this should be done as soon as they are noticed. Ectoparasites in a reptile collection are a sign of laziness in the keeper and there is no excuse for their presence.

Finally, infectious diseases can and do occur in snakes

and the most common of these are described on page 77. It should, however, be remembered that this book is just a guide and if any serious problem occurs the advice of a veterinarian should be sought straight away.

Sloughing Problems

Snakes in the wild almost never experience any problems while sloughing, except on rare occasions when they have suffered a physical injury to the skin which interferes with the normal progress of slough. If hampered in this way, such individuals normally perish as prey before too long. The reasons, then, why so many captive snakes suffer from sloughing problems must reflect on the way in which they are kept.

The first cause to be considered is a possible lack of humidity in the cage. Although the main substrate should always be kept completely dry, the cage should contain an area of water in which the snake can bathe, and it will often make use of this prior to sloughing. The presence of such a water area will also mean that there is a reasonable amount of humidity in the cage air. If a snake continually has problems while sloughing, simply spraying it lightly with lukewarm water in the early stages may help. Another possible solution in such a case might be to place in the cage a sealed container of damp moss with a hole cut in the top just large enough for the snake to be able to crawl in through.

Probably the second most likely cause of problems with sloughing is a lack of suitable objects against which the snake can rub. This can easily be rectified by placing suitable items such as branches, rocks and even plants in the vivarium. In such cases the above-mentioned tub of moss may also be useful.

Finally, if the snake's environmental needs are all correct, its physical condition must be taken into account. It may be that the snake is overweight and has grown lazy in captivity. In such cases snakes often make only a token effort to remove their own skins and wait for assistance, and there is then little option for the keeper but to keep removing the skin by hand as any which is left on for any length of time provides the perfect environment for the growth of bacteria. In such instances it would be beneficial to review the snake's diet. Alternatively the cause of the problem could be that the snake is underweight and in poor physical condition, perhaps as a result of endoparasites, disease or prolonged lack of appetite in an individual which has not adjusted well to captivity. The skin of a snake in this state should be removed gently by hand and steps taken to improve its health.

If a snake has received a physical injury to the skin such as a burn or a cut, it is probable that this will form a scab and will interfere with the sloughing process. Again there is little to remedy this problem other than careful removal by hand of each sloughing.

Assisting Sloughing

Helping a snake to slough can be done to different degrees from helping slightly to carefully removing the skin completely by hand. If the snake is newly acquired or has not experienced problems before, it is best to give it as little help as possible to begin with to see how much it is capable of doing for itself.

The simplest way to do this is to place the snake in a slightly damp cotton bag (which allows it to breathe) and leave the bag in the vivarium or somewhere suitably warm. This should provide the necessary high humidity, and the damp cotton should prove ideal for the snake to rub against. Leave the snake for about half an hour before checking it.

If the snake is still having problems after this time, the next step is to cover one hand with a damp hand cloth and allow the snake to crawl through it. Provided the old skin has not become too dry, allowing the snake to crawl through a reasonably firm grip should loosen much of it. After the snake has crawled through four or five times, most of the old skin, particularly that on the lower body, should have come free of the snake.

If all these steps fail, the skin should be removed by hand before any bacteria are allowed to take hold. The snake should be held gently but firmly by one person by the back of its head and lower body, and if possible the main part of the body should be supported by resting it on top of a table. A second person can then begin to remove any loose skin from the lower body, and areas of old skin which are not yet loose can be gently rubbed to loosen them but rubbing should always be done from the head to the tail end of the body. When working on the lower body it is important to check that the vent is not blocked. Removing skin from around the head should obviously be done very carefully, with rubbing always from the front to the back of the head. Special attention should be paid to ensure that the outer eye lenses come off with the rest of the skin and if they don't they should be rubbed with extreme care. If you are new to herpetology and are in doubt about carrying out any part of this operation, assistance should be sought from a local veterinarian, zoo or via one of the herpetological societies, most of which will be able to provide someone who can be of assistance.

Dietary Problems

Dietary problems in snakes are relatively rare as most species in captivity are fed on whole prey animals which provide a well-balanced diet with little need for any supplement. Garter Snakes, however, being so easy to convert to a diet of strips of processed fish, can be subject to dietary problems, but as long as care is taken to prepare the fish properly and vary the diet to include a variety of different prey items, these troubles should be few and far between. If for any reason a dietary problem does occur, the advice of a veterinarian who is experienced with herptiles should be sought. There are many commercially produced multi-vitamin powders available but these cover trace elements of most vitamins in order to improve balance and are not in themselves capable of reversing a serious imbalance in the diet. Instead a more concentrated preparation intended to correct a specific imbalance should be used under veterinary instruction until the snake is restored to health.

Vitamin B1 (thiamine) deficiency is still probably the

most common source of dietary problems in captive Garter Snakes in spite of much improved understanding of its cause and treatment over the course of recent years. As already mentioned (see page 64), the condition is caused by the use of thawed frozen fish as the major food supply. In such cases extra thiamine in the form of thiamine hydrochloride can be given by a vet, but this whole problem can generally be avoided so long as all frozen fish is heated at around 80°C for about five minutes before being offered to the 'patient'.

Steatitis, also often seen in captive Garter Snakes, is a deficiency of vitamin E which is most commonly the result of a diet of oily fish which leads to excessive levels of unsaturated fatty acids in the body. Over a period of time these will result in abnormally large deposits of fat, the skin covering them often becoming discoloured slightly with a yellow-to-orange pigmentation. To minimize the chances of this condition becoming a problem the snake's diet should be varied to include earthworms, other invertebrates and Pink Mice. Extra vitamin E can be added to the diet, and there are commercial products available for use with highly piscivorous animals, such as penguins and marine mammals, which may be useful in small quantities to snakes.

Calcium deficiency, or rickets as it is widely known, is not actually due to a straightforward deficiency of calcium in the diet but is more commonly caused by an imbalance of the calcium/phosphorus levels, in which calcium, which should normally predominate, is replaced by phosphorus as the dominate mineral. This can lead to a wide range of different bone development problems, the best-known forms perhaps being a deformed or hunched spine and a rubbery or broken jaw bone. Variety in the diet can help to prevent this deficiency, but it is best to include extra calcium in powdered form sprinkled on to the food from time to time, in addition to the more generalized multi-vitamin preparations which are given daily on the food.

The three conditions described above are the main dietary problems in the captive Garter Snake, but care should also be taken to ensure that the snake does not become overweight through an excess of food being available, combined with a lack of suitable exercise. In such cases it is also common for the snake to become slightly constipated. The obvious solution to this is simply to regulate the amount of food available to the snake and encourage it to exercise more. If a snake does appear to be mildly constipated, swimming in a shallow bath of warm water is an excellent form of exercise that will usually ease the trouble and prevent it from recurring in the future.

Physical Injuries (Trauma)

Cases of varying types of trauma are particularly common in newly imported specimens which have suffered poor treatment during capture and subsequent transportation, which is often followed by bad housing and husbandry prior to their sale. Trauma may also occur when the snake is introduced to a new vivarium it is not used to, or may be caused by other cage inhabitants which may not readily accept the newcomer. Care should always be taken when receiving new snakes or moving existing ones to avoid the possible types of trauma described below.

Abrasions, particularly to the front of the head, are common in many recently wild-caught snakes which do not accept confinement and spend the day rubbing against the sides of their enclosure looking for a possible source of escape. It should also be remembered that in their wild state they will not have been familiar with glass and so, on first encountering this material, will often hit up against it with force while trying to pass through it, thus risking injury. In such cases the area around the vivarium should be kept as quiet as possible to prevent the snake being suddenly scared and flying against the sides of its enclosure in trying to escape. The snake should eventually settle, but hiding areas within the enclosure should be increased until it can find one with which it feels secure.

If abrasions do occur they could become the source of a variety of secondary infections which may afflict the snake. To prevent this any injuries should be gently cleaned with hydrogen peroxide or a similar agent on the advice of a vet, and an appropriate antibiotic ointment should be applied until the problem has cleared.

Thermal burns resulting from direct contact with the cage heating or lighting equipment can and do happen from time to time. While normally any heating equipment in the cage is the subject of stringent safety care, with barriers always preventing direct contact between the snake and the heat source, problems often can arise when the light source is overlooked as a possible source of thermal burns. Light bulbs are most commonly the cause of accidents if they are positioned too close to cage furnishings or similar objects. While, for most of the time, the snake will not coil around such a hot object, at night when the bulb is cool the snake may well use it as a resting place from which it can reach and explore the roof of the vivarium looking for a possible area of escape. When therefore the time comes to switch on the light in the morning a check should always be made that the snake is not actually resting on the bulb as this will heat up before the snake has had enough time to sense the heat and move away without injury.

Minor burns should be treated with the application of a moist, sterile dressing, and antibiotics should also be administered. A serious burn, however, should be the subject of immediate veterinary inspection as the snake is likely to need the administration of electrolyte replacement fluid to prevent renal damage. Snakes which have suffered burns are usually left with scars which may later cause problems at times of sloughing; in such cases it is normally necessary to remove areas of old skin around the scar very gently by hand if the snake is to complete the shedding process without problems.

Bites between cage inmates do occasionally occur but these are usually fairly minor events with no serious consequences. If the area of a bite does, however, seem to become infected or a cyst or abscess starts to appear, veterinary advice should be sought.

The final group of commonly occurring traumas are those resulting from accidental crushing by loose vivarium furniture such as rocks or branches. Any hiding places provided for snakes should be of a rigid structure but, given a snake's ability to squeeze into and through the smallest of gaps, accidents can occur in even the best-designed vivariums. In such cases, if the snake is still alive when discovered, immediate veterinary attention should be sought to establish what if any damage has been done to the skeleton, particularly the spine. Because of their structure, snakes are remarkably resilient against such injuries but when they do occur they can be very difficult to treat because of the obvious problems in trying to restrict movement of the affected areas.

Parasites

Wild-caught snakes can carry a host of varying parasites for many years, often without any obvious ill effect. Such parasites can, however, be the source of many secondary infections which may have a more serious effect on the snake's health. Also, if the parasites are present in large numbers they may start to aggravate the deterioration of health in a specimen that has adjusted poorly to captivity and is not eating or drinking properly. These parasites divide roughly into two main groups. Ectoparasites are those that live on the exterior of the animal, such as ticks and mites which gain their nourishment by burrowing into the soft skin underneath the scales. Endoparasites live inside the host's body, frequently in the digestive tract, and most forms are referred to as varying types of 'worms'. Both of these main types of parasites can usually be easily eradicated and, where possible, every effort should be made to get rid of them. Ectoparasites in particular can, if given the chance, spread a secondary infection extremely rapidly through a collection of snakes, sometimes with devastating results.

Ectoparasites, which are nearly always in the form of either ticks or mites (see Fig. 17), are very common in captive snakes and will almost certainly be encountered by a snake keeper sooner or later. Ticks are the larger of the two, being about 3mm in length and grey to brown in colour. They have hook-type mouthparts with which

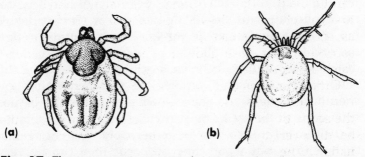

(a)   (b)

Fig. 17. The two common external parasites that frequently infest snakes: **(a)** the tick, and **(b)** the mite (not to scale).

they attach themselves firmly to the host. They can be removed manually, but before this is done they should be dabbed with a swab soaked in alcohol so that they loosen their grip on the host; otherwise they might be pulled off with the mouthparts left imbedded in the host so opening the way for possible infection.

Mites by comparison are much smaller and cannot be removed individually. They can be seen as small, black creatures moving over the skin of the snake. The easiest way to deal with them is to place in the vivarium a strip of Vapona or similar dichlorvos-containing pest strip, housed in a sealed container with ventilation holes to prevent the snake coming into direct contact with it. It is also important that the water container is removed while the Vapona is in the cage: the snake should be removed periodically and offered water outside the cage. In severe infestations the snake should be transferred to a sterile, unfurnished tank while its main cage is fumigated so as to kill any infestation in the substrate that could re-infest the snake once it has been treated.

Endoparasites, normally found in the form of parasitic worms inside the host's body, are extremely common in wild-caught snakes and can often be detected in the faeces. While their direct affect is not too dramatic, if present in large numbers they may weaken the host and there is always the risk of these worms carrying secondary infections. The most commonly encountered forms of endoparasite in snakes seem to be Roundworms and Tapeworms, but most types of intestinal parasitic worm can be dealt with by worming every snake newly added to a collection with 50–100mg of Panacur (Fenbendazole) as soon as the snake is received and administering a second similar dose about two weeks later in order to catch a second cycle of eggs hatching.

Other parasites, such as types of *Protozoa*, may be carried in the host's organs or blood supply but are beyond the scope of the snake owner to detect, though they may be discovered by a vet in a thorough medical examination. There is no usual treatment against such infestations unless they appear to be creating a problem.

Infectious Diseases

It is beyond the scope of this book to include all possible diseases that may afflict captive snakes and describe their treatment. Instead warning signs to watch out for are described, details of routine control to minimize the spread of infections are given and some of the most commonly encountered problems are explained. It is important, however, once an owner is aware that there is a problem, that veterinary advice is sought while there is time to treat the snake. All wild animals hide signs of poor health in order to remain competitive in the wild, so if ill health can be seen the problem must then be quite advanced and the need for treatment more urgent than at first may appear.

Signs of ill health vary but can include laboured and disturbed breathing, nasal or oral discharge, lack of or laboured movement and signs of discomfort in regions such as the mouth or areas of skin. Commonly the first sign is a lack of appetite, although this on its own may be caused by other factors such as the approach of an impending slough or changes in the environment of the enclosure. Having established that there is indeed a problem and having made arrangements to see a vet, the owner should be aware of the sort of questions the vet might ask and be ready to answer them accurately. Such questions may include: 'How long has the snake been owned?'; 'How long ago were the first signs of poor health noted?'; 'Is the snake kept on its own?'; 'Are other snakes kept elsewhere in the house?'; 'When did the snake last eat?'; 'Has there been any change in the food or water source?'; 'Has the snake been the subject of any medication or has an insecticide strip been used near it?' 'Has the cage been subject to any environmental changes such as photoperiod or temperature?'; and finally 'Has any unusual behaviour been noted?'

If an infectious disease is diagnosed, the owner should be ready to take steps to minimize any risk of infection to other reptiles which are kept in the same house. These steps should include: quarantining any snakes showing signs of poor health in separate individual cages, preferably in a different room from the main collection; not receiving snakes from other collections or sending any out; making sure all food and water containers are sterilized and not moved from one cage to another; making sure cages are kept as clean as is at all possible; ensuring that any waste material or dead bodies are removed quickly and sealed in a plastic bag before going for examination or incineration; and finally keeping the cage lighting and temperature as constant as possible in order to prevent unduly weakening the snake or aiding progress of the infection. Finally, as a matter of routine, any sick or ailing snakes should not be attended to until after the main collection has been serviced, so that there is no need once the ailing snake has been attended to return to the cage of a healthy specimen and so risk possible infection. With these simple steps and with veterinary assistance, most problems can be overcome.

Stomartitis, or mouth canker, is caused by a bacterium commonly present in cages and households without causing harm. Stomartitis can result, however, if the snake receives an injury to the interior of the mouth which becomes infected by the bacterium. The first signs of the condition are usually reluctance to eat and slight oversalivation. This is followed by inflammation of the oral mucous membranes, ulcers and the development of areas of necrosis which can be seen as yellowish, cheese-like lumps in the mouth. In the latter stages a foul smell can clearly be detected surrounding the animal's head. The treatment of this condition starts with a thorough but gentle cleaning of the interior of the mouth with a 3 per cent solution of hydrogen peroxide and any loose areas of necrosis should gently be removed. This cleaning of the mouth should be continued for at least ten days or until the infection is completely cleared. In addition to the cleaning, vitamin C can be given under veterinary supervision in a dosage of 10mg per kg of body weight. It should be noted that snakes suffering from this condition usually refuse to eat or drink, so it may be necessary to give small amounts of water daily via a catheter to badly afflicted specimens.

Respiratory diseases are most commonly encountered in snakes that are already in poor health, often as a result of being recently imported and subject to excessive over-crowding. Signs of respiratory disease are usually laboured breathing, sometimes with the mouth being opened, nasal discharge and excessive salivation. Such diseases are highly infectious, so any individual exhibiting signs such as these should be immediately quarantined and should be seen by a vet who will probably prescribe a course of antibiotics. Again it is important that the environment in which the snake is living is kept as stable as possible to minimize stress.

Fungal infections can appear on the scales of captive snakes, as can blistering if the main cage floor substrate is allowed to become damp and the snake cannot dry off properly. Should any blistering or fungal problems appear, the first step is to remove the snake to a completely dry environment. Then, if the trouble does not clear up within a reasonable period, veterinary assistance should be sought.

Breeding

The necessity of breeding snakes which are kept in captivity has already been mentioned in the Introduction. There are already present in captivity enough examples of many species to form a self-sustaining captive population to supply demand without any further removal of snakes from the wild. If captive breeding is to be attempted, the first and most obvious step is to ensure that you have two snakes of the same sub-species but of opposite sex.

Sexing

Correct sexing in mature Garter Snakes is a much easier exercise than in many other groups of snakes because, in most *Thamnophis* species, the female is noticeably larger and more robust in build than the male. In cases where this is not directly obvious, the normal methods of snake sexing are also applicable. The tail in male snakes is slightly longer than in the female, resulting in

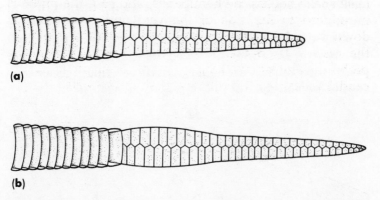

(a)

(b)

Fig. 18. The tails of **(a)** a female and **(b)** a male snake. Note the longer length of tail in the male and also the swelling at the base of the male's tail.

an increased number of sub-caudal scales in the male.
The male also has a swelling directly behind the cloaca
caused by the inverted hemipenes which can also usually
be observed by external examination (see Fig. 18).

All these external signs can usually give a reasonably
accurate guide to the sex of the snake, but in cases where
this cannot be done satisfactorily or in a young snake,
where any differences are much less apparent, the subject can be probed. Sexing probes for snakes can be
obtained from several commercial firms; it would be
unwise to try to use any form of home-made probe as
this could well lead to serious injury to the snake. It
would also be unwise to try probing a snake without first
taking advice on how to do it correctly from an experienced herpetologist either via a zoo or herpetological
society. Indeed, many suppliers of probes will sell them
only to people with an appropriate letter from a zoo to
the effect that the person trying to purchase the probes
is capable of using them correctly.

Probes are usually sold in sets of several different sizes
along with guidelines as to the suitability of each one
for varying species of snake. When using a probe, first
lubricate it with petroleum jelly or a similar product and
then give it a quick dip in a mild antiseptic before using
it on the snake. As illustrated in Fig. 18, the tail of the
male snake houses the hemipenes, and so if the probe is
introduced to the side of the vent and gently moved
down the tail, it may penetrate a reasonable distance. In
the case of the female, which has no hemipenes, the
probe can enter only for the length of about four sub-
caudal scales, significantly less than in the male.

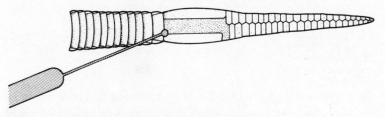

Fig. 19. Probing a snake to determine its sex.

When using the probe remember to be *extremely* gentle at all times, using the minimum of pressure. The probe should also be slowly rotated when in use as this helps to overcome problems such as the muscles in the hemipenes constricting and so giving a false result. Fig. 19 shows the use of a probe.

Stimulating Breeding

Having established that you do indeed have a true pair of snakes, the next consideration is how to recreate the seasonal variations that in nature stimulate breeding in wild populations of reptiles. As explained in Part One, the main climatic variations which affect snakes are the length of daylight hours and the average ambient daytime temperature. In captivity both factors can be easily controlled by the use of a time clock on the vivarium's lighting and by using a thermostat on the heating equipment.

The photoperiod within the vivarium should peak at around fourteen to fifteen hours in the summer months. Provided though, that the vivarium is in a well-lit room, as is usually the case, this period is often extended in summer by natural daylight. In the winter months a decrease in the numbers of hours of daylight should be

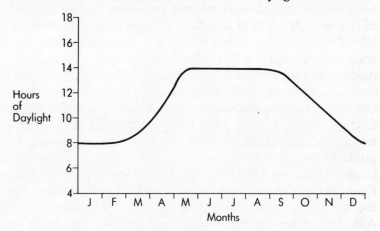

Graph 3. Recommended photoperiod over the course of a year.

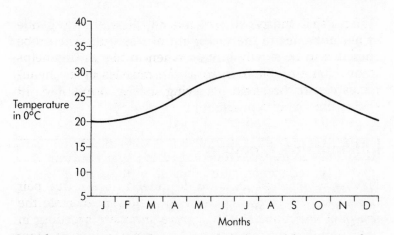

Graph 4. Recommended temperature cycle over the course of a year.

made along the lines illustrated in Graph 3. It is important, however, that this reduction is made gradually, with the daylight being reduced by no more than half an hour each week. Once the low of eight hours of daylight is reached, this level should be maintained for around six weeks before it is gradually increased again towards the summer level.

The change in the average ambient cage temperature is seen by most people as the more important factor of the two influencing breeding behaviour. I would disagree with this as it is almost certainly the correct combination of the two effects that is ultimately responsible in stimulating the snakes to breed. It is true, however, that variations in temperature have a more direct effect on snakes' health, so care should be taken that snakes that are not completely fit, that are suffering from chills or are generally underweight should not be subject to temperature fluctuations as these could weaken their health further and open the way for opportunist infections to follow. A guide to the appropriate temperature drop is provided in Graph 4, but the most important feature is that it mirrors the effect of the photoperiod so that both start and reach the bottom of their respective cycles at the same time. Any reductions in the temperature should also be at a very slow rate as sudden drops may adversely affect the snakes, particularly their digestion. In spring, however, when it comes to increasing the levels of light and temperature both can be increased at a slightly quicker rate than that at which they were reduced as this rapid change and the affect it has on snakes' hormones provides the main conditioning necessary to help them reproduce (see Graphs 3 and 4).

When snakes are experiencing periods of low temperature and reduced photoperiod, it is usual that they dramatically reduce or stop altogether their food intake. Therefore it is important that in late summer they are allowed to feed heavily, as many instinctively try to. Once they have become used to being cycled each year, they will defiantly seek in the latter part of the summer to put on weight ready for the coming winter.

With the correct environmental stimulation, then, it should not be long before mating takes place and pregnancy hopefully follows. It is not usually necessary to remove the male from the vivarium during pregnancy, but if it is a small vivarium or if the male is unduly disturbing the female it might then become advisable to do so. In the latter stages of pregnancy, when the swelling that has become evident in the lower abdomen of the female is first seen to start moving back through the body towards the cloaca, thought should be given as to where the female may give birth and a suitable area provided in advance so that she has plenty of time to get used to it and feel secure there. Young snakes are born covered with a sticky membrane sac, and if they are on a dry substrate they can suffer from the problem of drying out before releasing themselves from this sac. They may even become stuck to dry substrates such as newspaper or gravel. To avoid this a container of moist moss or a similar medium should be provided for the mother to use as a birth place. A 2-litre plastic ice-cream container with one corner of the lid removed serves this purpose extremely well; the lid provides the extra security essential to the snake immediately prior to giving birth.

Rearing

When the young snakes are born it is best to remove them from the main vivarium as the presence of the adults seems to intimidate them and prevent them wandering freely in search of food. A second small vivarium should therefore be set up ready – it should not be too large, otherwise the young snakes may not easily encounter food. The substrate on the floor of the small vivarium should be similar to that of the adults' but should contain many more hiding places for the young snakes to use. An area of moist moss at one end of the tank may be advantageous, and water should be provided in an extremely shallow dish for the first couple of days. If such a container cannot be found for the water, a larger one can be used but filled with pre-sterilised gravel to reduce any possibility of accidental drowning.

Food for the newly born snakes is not vastly different from that of the adults but simply of a much smaller size. White Worms are readily available and should be acceptable; small earthworms are readily eaten if they can be obtained in sufficient amounts; small Sand Eels and fine slices of fish can also be given and are soon taken. Other food items which may prove useful are small Tebo Bugs and Wax Worms, both of which are now commercially available to the hobbyist.

As the young grow there will be marked differences in the speed of growth of individuals if all are housed together as some assume dominance. As this starts to happen the young should be separated out so that only those of the same size and competitiveness are housed together. It may well be of advantage, if a large number of young are being reared at one time, to keep simple record cards (see the example illustrated on page 86) for each snake on top of their vivariums. These can record what food is being offered, if it is being eaten, sloughing dates and any other significant behaviour which may well also be useful to anyone obtaining the snake from you at a later date – they can see at a glance what the snake prefers to eat and how often it is used to being fed. Standard multi-vitamin preparations can be given to the

Example of a
Neonate Record Card

Species	Date of birth	Abnormalities		
T. sirtalis	24/8/89	None		
Date	Food offered	Eaten?	Slough	Observations
27/8 29/8 2/9	Earthworm Sand Eel	Yes No	 Slough	 Slight assistance
4/9 4/9	Strip of fish Earthworm	No Yes		Still reluctant to eat fish produce

young snakes with their food, and extra calcium in small quantities is also recommended. Otherwise young snakes grow well and usually encounter few problems. The age at which they reach sexual maturity varies but can be in their second year if they grow at a good rate.

Captive-bred snakes can provide better pets for people as they usually lose much of their fear and show more inquisitiveness than wild-caught specimens. They are also much more at home with vivarium life and so can make better future breeding stock. Disposal of young, therefore, is not likely to prove a problem: advertisements in herpetological literature should produce plenty of replies and this can prove a good way to meet people and make new friends with similar interests.

Part Three

Species of Garter and Ribbon Snakes

Identification Key to *Thamnophis Species*

The majority of Garter Snakes kept as pets are of a few common and recognizable types and there is usually little confusion in identifying them. Snakes which are encountered in the wild can be more difficult to identify, but by looking at which sub-species occur in that region one can normally get an accurate idea.

Snakes in captivity are more difficult to identify, especially if there is little or no information available about their past. Given that all *Thamnophis* species are of a broadly similar size and shape and also considering that body colouration can be very variable, even in snakes of the same sub-species, then it is not difficult to see why there is some confusion in identifying snakes of this genus.

Given below is an identification key that can be used to identify all *Thamnophis* species that can be found in the United States of America. To use the key, which is basically a series of questions, each question should be answered and according to which answer is correct the key will give the number of the next relevant question. The correct identification is eventually made through a process of elimination.

All species of the *Thamnophis* genus are small, lightly built snakes which all have keeled scales and all but one have a single anal plate. The key below is for the correct identification of full species; descriptions of sub-species are given later in the species descriptions.

1 (a) Back and side stripes normally absent, scales across the back are in 21 rows. There are 6 rows of numerous small dorsal spots; the eye is above the 5th or 5th and 6th upper labials. The lowest post-ocular encroaches on the orbitolabial contact; there are 8 upper labial scales; 2–3 pre-ocular scales; 3 post-ocular scales; 161–77 ventral scales; 69–87 caudal scales. = *T. rufipunctatus.*

(b) Side stripes and back stripe present; spots if present in 4 rows or fewer. →2

2 (a) Light side stripe involving scale rows 3 and 4. →3

(b) Light side stripe on scale row 3 only. →8

(c) Light side stripe on scale rows 2 and 3. →9

3 (a) Tail measures more than 0.27 of total length. →4

(b) Tail measures less than 0.27 of total length. →5

4 (a) Scales in 19 rows, 7 upper labials with the eye over 4th and 5th labials. Strongly marked back and side stripes. = *T. sauritus*

(b) Scales in 19 rows but has 8 upper labial scales. = *T. proximus*

5 (a) Side stripe on the 2nd, 3rd and 4th scale rows; upper labials 6–7 scales, small head that merges with body. Eye over the 3–4 labial scales. →6

(b) Side stripe on scales rows 3–4, upper labials scales number 7–9, scales in 21 rows. →7

6 (a) Scales in 17 rows, 6 upper labial scales. = *T. brachystoma*

(b) Scales in 19 rows, 7 upper labial scales. = *T. butleri*

7 Scales in 21 rows, 7 upper labial and 9 lower labial scales, eye over 4–5 labial scales. = *T. radix*

8 Scales in 21 rows, side stripe on the third scale row only. There are 8 upper labial scales and 6 rows of dorsal spots running down the body. Ventrals 155; caudals 70–4. = *T. marcianus*

9 (a) 7 upper labial scales. →10

 (b) 8 upper labial scales. →11

10 (a) Scales in 17 rows, ventrals usually less than 153; 8–9 lower labials, bright back stripe but side stripes are faint or absent. = *T. ordinoides*

 (b) Scales in 19 rows, ventrals usually more than 153; 10 lower labials, large eye. = *T. sirtalis*

11 (a) Prominent black nuchal spot clearly visible, scales are in 19 rows; there are 6 rows of dorsal spots. There are 8 upper labials of which the 6–7 are enlarged. = *T. cyrtopsis*

 (b) No prominent nuchal spot, dorsal spots if prominent in 4 rows; 8 upper labial scales with the 6–7 scales not being enlarged. = *T. couchi*

12 (a) Scales in 19–21 rows, inter-nasal scales are pointed at front; 8 upper labial scales with the 6–7 enlarged. = *T. elegans*

 (b) Scales in 19–21 rows, 8–9 upper labials but with the 6–7 not enlarged. No distinct pointing of the inter-nasal scales, large paired black spots at the back of the head. The anal plate is divided. = *T. eques*

Short-headed Garter Snake
(Thamnophis brachystoma)

Maximum length 56cm. The Short-headed Garter Snake, one of the smaller examples of the genus, is sometimes confused with the Eastern Garter Snake. The general colour is light greyish-brown, becoming darker higher up the back. A light greenish-yellow stripe runs down the arch of the back from the neck, fading out towards the end of the tail. Side stripes also run the length of the body along the 2nd, 3rd and 4th scale rows. These tend to be tipped with a faint black edging. This species is distinct from the Eastern Garter Snake in that it lacks the double row of black dorsal spots of the latter species. Scales across the body are in 17 rows, ventral scales can number between 132 and 146. Sub-caudal scales are usually around 68 in number in the male and around 60 in the female. The most noticeable feature of this species is the small and narrow shape of the head, which merges into the neck.

The main populations of this species are in north-west Pennsylvania and in the extreme south-west of New

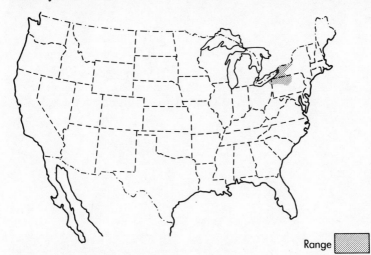

Range

Distribution of Short-headed Garter Snake.

York State. Some introduced populations exist in the Erie, Allegheny, and Butler Counties. It is most commonly encountered in meadows and damp grasslands, always in close proximity to areas of water and not so much in drier woodlands where the similar Eastern Garter Snake is more commonly found. The main food supply in the wild is probably earthworms, leeches and smaller amphibians. Mating normally occurs in April and May with up to fifteen young being born in mid-September. The young measure around 15cm in length.

Butler's Garter Snake
(Thamnophis butleri)

Maximum length 70cm. The Butler's Garter Snake is another species which could easily be confused with the Short-headed Garter Snake but can be identified by the number of rows of scales that run across the back. While the Short-headed Garter Snake has 17 rows, the Butler's Garter Snake has 19 over most of the forebody, although these become 17 towards the tail. It has a simple but

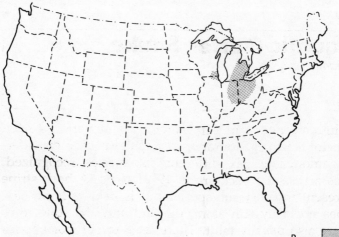

Range

Distribution of Butler's Garter Snake.

attractive overall body colour of brownish-black with three yellow stripes running the length of its body, one along the arch of the back from the neck down towards the base of the tail and the other two down the sides mainly along the 3rd scale row although the stripes also cross over to the 2nd and 4th rows. Depending on how dark the main body colouring is, there may also be lines of black spots present between these stripes. Ventral scales usually number between 130 and 147 with the sub-caudal scales averaging around 64 in male snakes and 56 in females. Upper labial scales usually number 7.

The Butler's Garter Snake can be found in the southern part of Ontario, east of Michigan, east of Indiana and west of Ohio. It is mainly encountered in damp meadows and grasslands or near marshes and streams in open areas. The prey in the wild is thought to include earth-worms, leeches, small frogs and salamanders, although in captivity the snake can prove to be a choosy feeder, often accepting only earthworms to begin with and some-times even refusing those. Mating normally takes place in March to April with young being born in late summer. Up to 16 young can be born, although 8–10 is the most common number. The young measure around 14–18 cm at birth and take up to three years to mature.

Aquatic Garter Snake
(Thamnophis couchi)

Maximum length can vary among the sub-species from 45cm to 145cm. Colouration and pattern vary consider-ably among the six different sub-species recognized. Scales across the back are in 19–21 rows. A back stripe is present in most sub-species but is usually faint; side stripes normally run along the 2nd and 3rd scale rows but are also usually faint. There are 8 upper labial scales and the inter-nasal scales are slightly pointed towards the front. All sub-species of the Aquatic Garter Snake are

Range

Distribution of Aquatic Garter Snake.

found in the region from south-west Oregon down to Baja, California, and from the Californian coast inwards to west Nevada.

The **Sierra Garter Snake** (*Thamnophis couchi couchi*). The main body colour is dull yellow which is chequered with darker blotches. There is usually a narrow black stripe running down the back, although this becomes faint towards the back of the body. Side stripes can also be present, but these are not very clear, being a dull yellow in colour. Scales are normally in 21 rows; pre-ocular scales are often divided. This sub-species is found in the Sierra Nevadas in California and in Nevada.

The **Coast Garter Snake** (*Thamnophis couchi aquaticus*), as its scientific sub-species name suggests, is probably the most aquatic in lifestyle of the various sub-species. It has a distinctive wide yellow stripe running the length of its back, and there are also more subtle side lines on either flank. The main upper body colour varies from olive to dark brown, but the throat is light yellow with the under side also yellowish to lighter shades of bluish-green with darker blotching. Scales are normally in 19 rows, ventral scales range from 142 to 167 in number and sub-caudal scales average around 74 in females and 85 in males. This sub-species is from the San Francisco Bay area and inland to the Sacramento Valley.

The **Santa Cruz Garter Snake** (*Thamnophis couchi atratus*) has back and side stripes, although the side stripes that run along the 2nd and 3rd scale rows can be faint and visible only on handling in some individuals. There are frequently 2 rows of black alternating spots between the side and back stripes. The main colour of the snake is a dull brownish-black and unless it is handled overmarkings may be undetectable. The throat is light yellow, as in the Coast Garter Snake, but the two can easily be distinguished as the Santa Cruz Garter Snake has a bluish belly. There are 19 scale rows and the number of ventral scales can vary from 140 to 169; subcaudal average around 80 in males and 72 in females. This sub-species also comes from the San Francisco Bay area south to Monterey.

The **Giant Garter Snake** (*Thamnophis couchi gigas*), as its name suggests, is the largest of all Garter Snakes, commonly reaching lengths of up to 145cm. The main body colour is dull olive-brown. It has a back and side stripes which are a lighter yellowish-olive but these can be faint, usually merging into the main body colour with two rows of alternating black blotches on each side of the upper flanks giving the snake a more chequered appearance. Scale rows are usually 21–3, ventrals usually 165–70 and the head appears slightly elongated. This sub-species is found in the San Joaquin area in California from Sacramento down to Buena Vista Lake.

The **Two-striped Garter Snake** (*Thamnophis couchi hammondi*) is the only sub-species of *T. couchi* completely to lack any sign of a stripe along the centre of the back. It does, however, have noticeable yellow stripes running down the 2nd and 3rd scale rows. Above the side stripes may be a row of small black spots intermingled with yellow marks. The main body colour is light brown with the under side of the head and neck light yellow: this continues down the centre of the ventral scales where it darkens to orange-yellow. Scales are in 21 rows and the pre-oculars are split. This sub-species is found along coastal California from Monterey to Baja.

The **Oregon Garter Snake** (*Thamnophis couchi hydrophilus*) has a yellow back stripe but the side stripes are extremely faint or usually lacking altogether. The main body colour is grey with poorly defined alternating black spots, giving the snake a blotched appearance. Scale rows can vary from 21 to 19. This sub-species can be found from south-western Oregon south along the coast of northern California and inland to the Sacramento Valley region.

All of these sub-species of *T. couchi* are mainly aquatic in their lifestyle and are usually diurnal. The main food supply would appear to be fish, adult amphibians as well as their larvae and more occasionally leeches and earthworms. The breeding cycle also varies among the sub-species but usually from 10 to 25 young are born in late summer. The young are large and can measure anything up to 25cm, particularly in the case of *T.c. gigas*.

Black-necked Garter Snake
(Thamnophis cyrtopsis)

Maximum length 110cm. The main body colouration is dull, being dull grey to brown. The common name is derived from a black collar behind the skull that is divided only by the back stripe. The back stripe is orange, although this usually fades to yellow towards the tail; this stripe also becomes slightly broader in the region of the neck. There are two broad side stripes, occupying the 2nd and 3rd scale rows, which are usually light grey in colour. Two alternating rows of black spots run down along the length of the body between the back and the side stripes and can at times intrude into the side stripes, giving them a wavy appearance. The top of the head is grey, which becomes lighter down the sides. Scales are in 19 rows; ventrals average between 162 and 167. Much of the southern range of this species is shared with the Mexican Garter Snake (*T. eques*) which appears superficially very similar; they can, however, be easily distinguished as *T. eques* averages less than 162 ventral

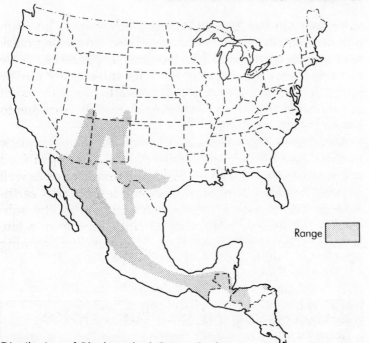

Distribution of Black-necked Garter Snake.

scales and has a distinctive split anal plate. Three sub-species are recognized, although this number is under review. This species is widely distributed in the southern central states of America, New Mexico and down into Central America. In the United States it occurs in southern Utah, south Colorado through to eastern Arizona, New Mexico and in the Transpeco, Big Bend and Edwards Plateau regions of Texas. In Mexico it occurs in Chihuahua, Coahuila, Durango, Nayarit, San Luis Potosi and Sonora, with the third sub-species reaching through Central America to Costa Rica.

The **Western Black-necked Garter Snake** (*Thamnophis cyrtopsis cyrtopsis*) is the nominate sub-species and is as described above. It is particularly noticeable in this race that the alternating black spots in the area around the neck are small and clearly defined. This sub-species can be found in south-eastern Utah and southern Colorado in the United States and reaching south into Mexico.

The **Eastern Black-necked Garter Snake** (*Thamnophis cyrtopsis ocellatus*) differs principally from the nominate sub-species by having single large black spots in the neck region which are much less well defined and because the side stripes have more of a scalloped appearance. This sub-species is found primarily in Texas in the area from Edwards Plateau west to the Big Bend.

The **Southern Black-necked Garter Snake** (*Thamnophis cyrtopsis fulvus*) differs from the preceding sub-species by having a more brownish-coloured head and a much-reduced number of ventral scales, usually between 132 and 154. It can still easily be distinguished from the Mexican Garter Snake by means of its single anal plate. This sub-species is unlikely to become available as it occurs mainly in Mexico and Honduras. It is also the subject of much debate as to its correct taxonomy, many people now describing it as a full species of *Thamnophis* – *Thamnophis fulvus*.

This species in its varying forms is usually found in more arid regions than other Garter Snakes, with fir or pine forests proving a favoured environment. They can also be found in sparsely vegetated areas around desert flats but only if within reasonable distance of a stream or similar area of water. The main prey are amphibians which are encountered in or around the water area. The species is diurnal in its habits and can frequently be seen during the day hunting or basking on rocks overhanging the water. As with all *Thamnophis* species, Black-necked Garter Snakes give birth to live young normally from July to August. Up to 25 young can be born at once, measuring 20–25cm at birth.

Western Terrestrial Garter Snake
(Thamnophis elegans)

Maximum length 106cm. Descriptions among the sub-species vary but colouration is normally quite dull. There are side stripes which occupy the 2nd and 3rd scale rows and there is also a back stripe but all three are variable as to how well defined they are. The space between the back and side stripes can be marked with dark spots or light flecking. The inter-nasal scales are not pointed in front. Scale rows can number either 19 or 21; ventral scales average 167 and sub-caudal 57. As the common name suggests, the main populations of this species come from the western states of America reaching down into Mexico, with five differing sub-species being recognized.

The **Mountain Terrestrial Garter Snake (*Thamnophis elegans elegans*)** is the nominate sub-species. It has quite

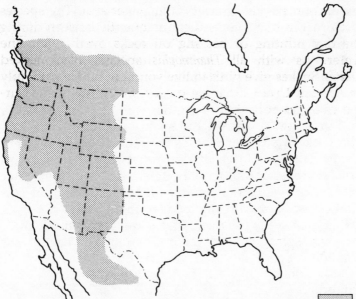

Distribution of Western Terrestrial Garter Snake.   Range

clearly defined back and side stripes with the back stripe being light orange in colour and the side stripes a dull grey. The ventral surface is plain pale grey with no marking. It has 21 rows of scales. This sub-species can be found in western Nevada, the Sierra Nevada, on the coastal mountain ranges of California and in the Cascade Mountains of west Oregon.

The **Klamath Terrestrial Garter Snake** (*Thamnophis elegans biscutatus*) is similar to the nominate sub-species and also has a conspicuous back stripe, although in this sub-species it is yellow. The ventral surface is still basically grey but is much darker, appearing to be washed with black. This sub-species has 21 rows of scales and often has the pre-ocular scales divided in two. It occurs in southern Oregon and the extreme north-east of California.

The **Coastal Terrestrial Garter Snake** (*Thamnophis elegans terrestris*) is similar to the preceding sub-species and also has a wide yellow back stripe as its most distinctive feature. It does differ markedly on the ventral surface, however, by having distinctive red or orange flecking down the sides of the belly. As its common name suggests, this sub-species is mainly found along the western coast in south-western Oregon reaching down to Santa Barbara County in California.

The **Wandering Terrestrial Garter Snake** (*Thamnophis elegans vagrans*) is, as its name suggests, the most widespread sub-species. Unlike in the preceding sub-species the side and back stripes are not well marked and are a dull grey colour against the snake's basic brown body. The back stripe even merges in towards the tail. There are two rows of black markings between the back and side stripes but these, although clear, are somewhat random in their arrangement. The top of the head is a light brown but with darker markings behind the eyes and at the base of the neck. Scales are usually in 21 rows. This widespread sub-species can be found in south-west Manitoba, South Dakota, western Oklahoma across to British Columbia, western Washington, Oregon and California.

The **Mexican Terrestrial Garter Snake** (*Thamnophis*

elegans errans) is unlikely to become available as it does not occur in the United States. It has only a narrow back stripe with slightly wider side stripes. The most noticeable feature is a black collar which is much more distinct than in the Wandering Garter Snake (*T.e. vagrans*). This sub-species can be found only in Mexico.

All of the Terrestrial Garter Snakes are diurnal in habit and lifestyle, preferring moist habitats such as meadows, open grasslands, or the edges of ponds, lakes or streams. They are generally very opportunist feeders and will tackle any source of available prey they may encounter, such as fish, amphibians, earthworms, slugs and even lizards, young mammals or birds should the opportunity arise. Following spring matings, young are born between July and September. Up to 19 young may be born at once and these can measure up to 23cm at birth. Maturity can be reached in the second year but more usually from the third onwards.

Mexican Garter Snake
(*Thamnophis eques*)

Maximum length 102cm. A stoutly built species of *Thamnophis* with a basic body colouration of greenish-brown. There is a light yellow back stripe and similarly coloured side stripes running down the 3rd and 4th scale rows. These side stripes become less distinct towards the end of the body. There are some black markings between the back and side stripes which are small alternating spots but not well defined. There are two large black spots at the top of the neck, giving the snake a small black collar which can at first sight lead to some confusion with the Black-necked Garter Snake (*Thamnophis cyrtopsis*) which shares much of the Mexican Garter Snake's range. The ventral surface can be pale green, grey or blue but has dark spotting. This species is unique among *Thamnophis* in having the anal plate divided, making it easily ident-

Distribution of Mexican Garter Snake.

Range

ifiable. As its name suggests, this species is found primarily in Mexico and down into Central America, with just one of the three recognized sub-species reaching northwards into the United States as far as Arizona and New Mexico.

The **Common Mexican Garter Snake** (*Thamnophis eques eques*) is the nominate sub-species and is as described above. It is extremely widespread within Mexico but does not occur inside the United States and for this reason is unlikely to become available.

The **Northern Mexican Garter Snake** (*Thamnophis eques megalops*) varies little from the nominate race except that the main body colour is more of an olive-brown. This sub-species' range does extend into Arizona and New Mexico so it may become available infrequently. It is an attractive snake and although not widely kept should be relatively unproblematic to keep.

The **Durango Mexican Garter Snake** (*Thamnophis eques virgatenius*) is found only in the state of Durango in Mexico and as such is again unlikely to become available. It also varies little from the nominate.

The Mexican Garter Snake, in its three varying races, is mainly aquatic in lifestyle. It is also diurnal and can often be seen during the day hunting along the banks of streams, ditches, ponds or lakes which form its favourite habitat sites. Its principal prey source is frogs but it will also tackle other suitable aquatic food items it may encounter, such as small fish or leeches. Following spring mating, young may be born quite early – often in June – although sometimes not until August. Up to 25 young can be born from one pregnancy with each individual measuring around 24cm in length at birth.

Chequered Garter Snake
(Thamnophis marcianus)

Maximum length 108cm. The main body colour is olive-brown. There is a broad back stripe and side stripes on the 3rd scale row. The back stripe sometimes does not extend fully to the head, being blocked by a broad black collar at the top of the neck. There are two very vivid rows of alternating black spots running down the length of the body between the side and back stripes which give this snake its common name; these spots can and often do infringe on to the back and side stripes. A third row of spots can occasionally be seen but these tend to be faint and not well defined. The head is a lighter olive-brown and the chin and ventral surface are paler. Scales are in 21 rows with 8 upper labial scales; ventral scales average 155 or less and sub-caudal scales average 74 in males and 72 in females. Two sub-species are generally recognized which range from California across to Texas and south-west Kansas and reaching down to Costa Rica.

The **Northern Chequered Garter Snake** (*Thamnophis marcianus marcianus*) is the nominate sub-species and is as described above. This is the only form of Chequered

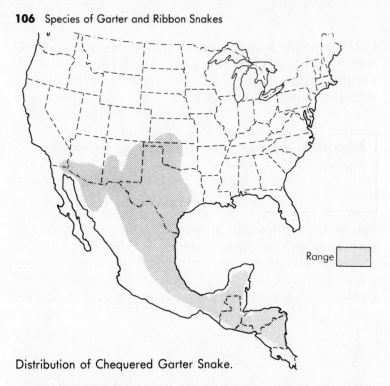

Distribution of Chequered Garter Snake.

Garter Snake likely to be available as it can be found in south-eastern California, southern Arizona, eastern and south-western New Mexico across to eastern Texas and north to south-western Kansas.

The **Southern Chequered Garter Snake** (*Thamnophis marcianus praecularis*) varies little from the nominate except that a third row of black spots under the side stripes may be visible. It also averages between 155 and 160 ventral scales, slightly more than in the nominate. This sub-species is unlikely to be available: it is known from Mexico, Belize, Honduras and Costa Rica.

Chequered Garter Snakes are most frequently found in arid and semi-arid grasslands near streams, ponds or irrigation ditches in the United States, while in comparison descriptions of habitat for *T.m. praecularis* mention sub-tropical, wet, forest-type habitats. They are mainly diurnal in their habits and lifestyle but are also often active on warm summer nights. Their main food source is aquatic prey such as amphibians and fish, but they take earthworms, small lizards and small mammals too.

Up to 18 young snakes measuring anything up to 24cm in length at birth are born usually between June to August, depending on what area of the range and climate the sub-species inhabits.

North-western Garter Snake
(Thamnophis ordinoides)

Maximum length 66cm. The main upper body colour can vary from greenish-brown through to black. The most noticeable feature at first sight is the deep reddish-orange colour of the back and two side stripes, which are all vividly marked and extremely attractive. Depending on

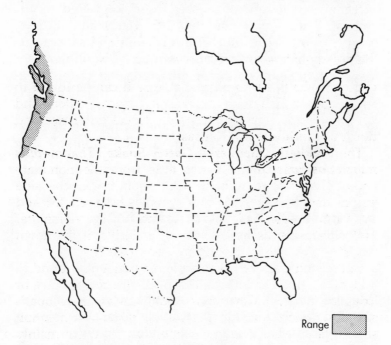

Range

Distribution of North-western Garter Snake.

the darkness of the upper body colour, there may also be two rows of black spots running down the body from head to tail between the side and back stripes. The chin is usually also reddish-orange, connecting with the side stripe on either side. The rest of the ventral surface is pale yellow with occasional orange blotching. Scales over the body are normally in 17 rows with 7 upper labial scales present. Ventrals average between 140 and 160 and the sub-caudal scales number on average 74 in males and 68 in females.

As its name suggests, this species comes from the north-west area of the United States, being found on Vancouver Island and the southern coastal region of British Columbia, western Washington, western Oregon and in the extreme north of California. Its preferred habitat is meadows and grasslands, especially if these areas contain streams, but it can to a lesser extent be found in any habitat within its range that has water and a ready supply of prey. It is diurnal in its habits and as such can frequently be encountered on warm days hunting on the edges of streams, ponds or other areas of water for its normal diet which may include small amphibians, leeches and earthworms and smaller fish. Early spring mating is recorded resulting in the birth of as many as 15 young which can measure up to 18cm, from late June through to August.

Western Ribbon Snake
(Thamnophis proximus)

Maximum length 123cm. As its common name suggests, the Ribbon Snake is a particularly slender species of *Thamnophis*. It has a simple colouration with well-defined back and side stripes contrasting sharply with the plain black body colour. The back and side stripes are usually of a light creamy yellow or light orange; the back stripe normally being of a slightly darker shade. The side

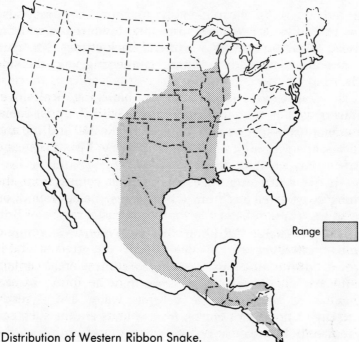

Distribution of Western Ribbon Snake.

stripes normally run down the length of the body along the 3rd and 4th scale rows. A distinctive feature of this species is the presence of two fused spots on the crown of the head. Scales across the body are in 19 rows; there are 8 upper labial scales with the eye normally situated over the 4th and 5th labial scales. This species is widespread in the central states of America and reaches down to Mexico and Costa Rica. In North America it occurs more westerly of the *T. sauritus* populations down the eastern states of America and is found in south Wisconsin, Indiana and the Mississippi valley, west to eastern Nebraska, south-east Colorado and east New Mexico and south right down into Central America.

The **Western Ribbon Snake (*Thamnophis proximus proximus*)**, the nominate sub-species, is as described above and is commonly seen. It can be found in the states of Indiana, south Wisconsin and eastern Nebraska south to southern Louisiana and north-eastern Texas.

The **Arid Land Ribbon Snake (*Thamnophis proximus diabolicus*)** differs mainly from the nominate sub-species by having a lighter olive-grey to brown upper body colour and a narrow dark stripe that borders the ventral scales. This sub-species is found from south-eastern Colorado and Kansas south through western Texas and into Mexico.

The **Gulf Coast Ribbon Snake (*Thamnophis proximus orarius*)** also has a generally lighter body colour than the nominate sub-species and a noticeably wider bright gold back stripe running the length of its body. Like the nominate it has no dark stripe bordering the ventral scales. As its name suggests, this sub-species is primarily found along coastal regions from the extreme south of Mississippi to southern Texas.

The **Red-striped Ribbon Snake (*Thamnophis proximus rubrilineatus*)** is olive-brown in general body colour but the most distinctive feature of this sub-species is the bright red back stripe. There may also be a narrow dark stripe bordering the ventral scales. This highly attractive sub-species comes from a limited range, being found only in areas of Texas.

There are two further sub-species which are highly unlikely to become available. *Thamnophis proximus rutiloris* has a brownish body colour with a light tan back stripe and yellowish-orange side stripes. It may also have a narrow dark line bordering the ventral scales. This sub-species is recorded from Mexico south to Costa Rica. *Thamnophis proximus alpinus* is still arguably distinct from *T.p. rutiloris* in that parietal spots on the head are chevron-shaped, unlike those of the latter.

Western Ribbon Snakes are diurnal in their habits and can often be found during the early morning and late afternoon foraging for food in favoured habitats such as vegetation surrounding ponds, lakes, streams or any covered area near a water supply. This species can frequently be seen sunbathing in grasses or reeds overhanging or close to the edge of water. The main food source is amphibians, but they will readily take fish, leeches, slugs and earthworms as well. After spring mating, as many as 27 young can be born from one litter, normally in the months between July and September. The young measure around 26cm at birth and can become mature in their third summer.

Plains Garter Snake
(Thamnophis radix)

Maximum length 102cm. The main upper body colour can vary from greyish-brown to reddish-orange. There is nearly always an extremely vivid yellow stripe that runs the length of the back. Side stripes are also present but these are less vivid, being a pale grey colour, and running mainly along the 3rd row of scales, though the line may occasionally cross on to the 4th row as well. Two well-defined rows of black spots run down the body between the side and back stripes and, interestingly, a third well-defined row of spots runs down the body below the side stripe. Another distinctive feature of the species is the presence of vertical black stripes on the labial scales. Scales across the body are in 21 rows, although there is a difference between the two sub-

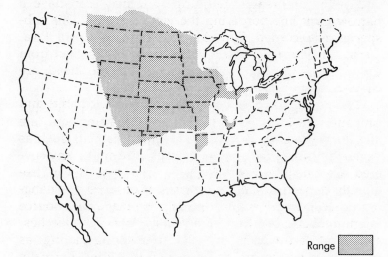

Range

Distribution of Plains Garter Snake.

species as to the number of rows of scales present across the neck. The number of ventral scales also varies slightly between the two sub-species but is usually around 155. The number of sub-caudal scales averages out at around 75 in male snakes and around 65 in females. Two sub-species are recognized, both getting their common name from the fact that they are found from north-west Indiana south through the Great Plains and Rockies to the north of New Mexico.

The **Eastern Plains Garter Snake** (*Thamnophis radix radix*), the nominate race, is coloured as described above and normally has less than 155 ventral scales as opposed to the Western sub-species which usually has more. It also has only 19 rows of scales reaching across its neck region. It occurs from north-western Indiana northwards to Canada and is also found in Iowa, Wisconsin, Missouri and Illinois.

The **Western Plains Garter Snake** (*Thamnophis radix haydeni*) differs little from the Eastern in colour, the main difference being that it has a full 21 rows of scales reaching across the neck region of the body and that the number of ventral scales usually averages more than 155. This sub-species is found widely in western Iowa, Minnesota and north-western Missouri west to the Rockies.

Both sub-species are similar in appearance and habits. They can normally be found in open, damp grasslands, wet meadows, drainage ditches or open areas along the edges of lakes or marshes. The main diet is small amphibians, leeches, earthworms and even small mammals. There is also more than one report of this species being observed eating carrion. It is diurnal in its lifestyle and can be seen hunting prey during the day. Mating is usually during the months of April and May, resulting in large broods of young: 20–30 in a single litter are common but up to 60 have been recorded. The young, measuring up to 19cm at birth, are most commonly born in the months from July through to September, usually reaching maturity after three years.

Narrow-headed Garter Snake

(Thamnophis rufipunctatus)

Maximum length 87cm. The Narrow-headed Garter Snake is perhaps one of the dullest-looking species of *Thamnophis* and probably the one that adapts least well to captivity. As its common name suggests, the shape of its head is more elongated than in other species. The main body colour is dull light brown. It has no back or side stripes but rather a series of ill-defined dark brown blotches running the length of its body which may join over the arch of the back to create a pattern of saddles down the back. Scales across its body are in 21 rows. When the side stripes are present they normally run down the 2nd and 3rd scale rows. There are 8 upper labial scales present.

The main populations of this snake are found in eastern Arizona to south-western New Mexico and in north-western Mexico. It is almost entirely aquatic in its habits, being found in streams in woodlands or forests. It will venture out of the water to bask on warm summer days

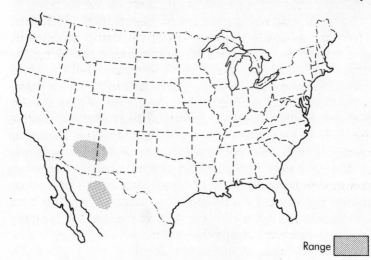

Range

Distribution of Narrow-headed Garter Snake.

but soon returns for cover if disturbed for it is extremely nervous and does not adjust as well to captivity as most of the other *Thamnophis* species do. The diet in the wild is almost exclusively fish and aquatic invertebrates.

Not a great deal is known about the breeding habits of this snake in the wild or in captivity, but young are generally first seen around July in the wild.

Eastern Ribbon Snake
(Thamnophis sauritus)

Maximum length 102cm. The two species of Ribbon Snakes are the most slender and agile of the Garter Snake group and their tails are usually noticeably longer. Colouration varies greatly among the four sub-species of the Eastern Ribbon Snake but most have clear, bright stripes down the back and along the sides running along the 3rd and 4th rows of scales which contrast with the darker body colours. Scales across the body are in 19 rows. As the common name of the nominate sub-species suggests, all sub-species inhabit the more easterly states of America.

The **Eastern Ribbon Snake** (***Thamnophis sauritus sauritus***) is the nominate sub-species and follows the general description well. It has clear, vivid back and side stripes. The back stripe is yellowish-orange while those on the side are a slightly lighter yellow. The main body colour can vary from reddish-brown to black, but is normally slightly lighter under the side stripe than above. If the upper body colour is a lighter shade, faint darker spots can be made out just above the side lines. This sub-species is found in south Indiana, southern and eastern Pennsylvania, the south-eastern part of New York State, the south of New Hampshire and widely across the states of Florida, Louisiana and South Carolina.

The **Blue-striped Ribbon Snake** (***Thamnophis sauritus nitae***) has a dark brown to black upper body with a less

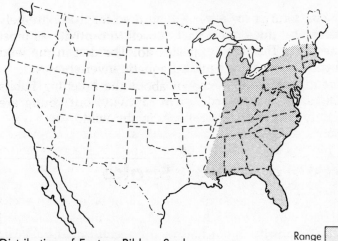

Distribution of Eastern Ribbon Snake.

Range

well-defined back stripe of a lighter brown colour. It gets its common name from the two narrow but extremely bright creamish-blue side stripes which run the length of its body; these connect to the chin which is also a light blue colour. This sub-species has a restricted home range along the gulf coast of Florida from the Withlacoochee River to Wakulla County.

The **Peninsula Ribbon Snake** (*Thamnophis sauritus sackeni*) is superficially similar to the aforementioned Blue-striped Ribbon Snake and overlaps most of its range. It does, however, lack the bright, light colour in the side lines of that sub-species. The main body colour is brown. The back stripe is a tan-brown colour while the side stripes are a light brown. This sub-species is found right across peninsula Florida and also in the south of Carolina and south-eastern Georgia.

The **Northern Ribbon Snake** (*Thamnophis sauritus septentrionalis*) has a dark brown to black upper body colour and is similar to the Eastern sub-species, having this dark colouration contrasting with three bright yellow stripes. While the side stripes are bright yellow, as in the Eastern, the back stripe does differ as the main yellow pigmentation is usually mixed with a darker brown colour. This sub-species can be found in Michigan, south Ontario, south Indiana, south Maine to the coast and around coastal New Hampshire and Pennsylvania.

Habitats for these snakes can vary from grasslands to marshes to the edges of larger water areas, but are always near the edge of water whether stream or lake. The snakes are semi-aquatic in their habits and are most commonly encountered basking on rocks and bushes which overhang water. When threatened they rapidly dive into the water and swiftly glide across the surface to safety. The diet of wild snakes is based mainly on amphibians and fish, although some invertebrate matter is probably also taken. Breeding behaviour is similar in all sub-species, with mating taking place in spring and up to 26 young measuring up to 23cm being born some time between July and August. As with most *Thamnophis* species, maturity is reached in the second or third year.

Common Garter Snake
(Thamnophis sirtalis)

With 12 sub-species spread right across America, this species is highly variable, maximum length ranging from 50 to 130cm. The colouration varies greatly between the sub-species but nearly all have well-defined back and side stripes. The side stripes in all sub-species except the Texas one (*T.s. annectans*) are confined to the 2nd and 3rd scale rows. There are usually markings between the side and back stripes made up of either spots or larger blotches of varying colours. There are 19 rows of keeled scales and normally 7 upper labial scales. Ventral scales normally number between 138 and 168 and sub-caudals average around 84 in male snakes and 58 in females.

The **Eastern Common Garter Snake** (***Thamnophis sirtalis sirtalis***) is the nominate sub-species. It normally has yellowish stripes, although these are absent in some specimens which are almost completely black. There are frequently double rows of spots between the side and back stripes, with colours varying from greenish-blue to brown. Populations of this sub-species are widespread

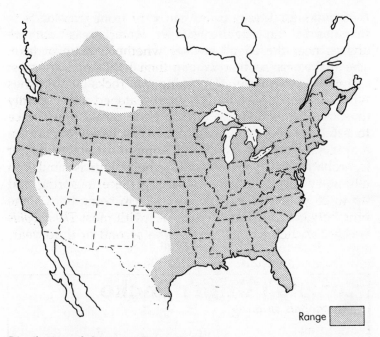

Distribution of Common Garter Snake.

from southern Ontario, eastern Minnesota and Iowa to southern Missouri and Arkansas; from Eastern Texas through to the Atlantic coast and from southern Newfoundland to the south of Florida.

The **Texas Common Garter Snake (*Thamnophis sirtalis annectans*)** has a back stripe which is broad and orange in colour. The side stripes run along the 3rd scale row but also reach on to the 2nd and 4th rows. The main population of this sub-species in found on the Oklahoma–Texas border running south through Texas, with an isolated population down in the Texas Panhandle.

The **Red-spotted Common Garter Snake (*Thamnophis sirtalis concinnus*)** is almost black with a vivid yellowish-grey stripe. The common name derives from the single row down each side of the body of large, well-defined, red spots. The upper part of the head is also marked with red. This attractive sub-species is confined to northwestern Oregon and the extreme south-west of Washington.

The **Valley Common Garter Snake (*Thamnophis sirta-***

lis fitchi) is dark grey to brown with a well-defined back stripe and the top of the head is black. This sub-species occurs in northern and coastal California, although it is absent from areas heavily populated by the Californian Red-sided sub-species (*T.s. infernalis*). It is also found in north-western Nevada, south-western and eastern Oregon, Idaho, Utah, western Montana and from Washington through British Columbia to south-eastern Alaska.

The **Californian Red-sided Common Garter Snake** (*Thamnophis sirtalis infernalis*) closely resembles the Red-sided sub-species (*T.s. parietalis*); it has a well-defined dark grey back stripe with less well-defined side stripes. There are red blotches running down the body above the side stripes and the top of the head is also red. This sub-species is found along the coastal edge of California from Humboldt County down to San Diego County.

The **New Mexico Common Garter Snake** (*Thamnophis sirtalis dorsalis*) also resembles the Red-sided sub-species but the red marking down the sides of the body is much reduced and mainly confined to the skin in between the scales rather than being on the scales themselves. It can be found in the Rio Grande valley and from the extreme south of Colorado through New Mexico to the extreme west of Texas.

The **Maritime Common Garter Snake** (*Thamnophis sirtalis pallidula*) is similar to the Eastern sub-species but the back stripe is faint or absent altogether; the spotting is also much more strongly defined. This snake occurs in the Canadian maritime provinces, mainly around Quebec, and in adjacent areas of New England.

The **Red-sided Common Garter Snake** (*Thamnophis sirtalis parietalis*) has a well-defined back stripe with much less well-defined side stripes. It has strongly marked red bars between the back and side stripes, which give it a highly attractive chequered appearance. The top of the head is usually olive-brown. This snake occurs in south-eastern British Columbia, Alberta and southern Manitoba south through the Great Plains to the Oklahoma–Texas border.

The **Puget Sound Common Garter Snake** (*Thamnophis sirtalis pickeringi*) resembles the Red-spotted sub-species but lacks these markings on its generally darker colouration and the back stripe is also narrower. The top of the head is generally dark in colour. It can be found on Vancouver Island and in adjacent coastal south-west British Columbia and western Washington.

The **Chicago Common Garter Snake** (*Thamnophis sirtalis semifasciatus*) is similar to the nominate sub-species but differs by having black vertical bars breaking through the side stripes in the region around the neck. It can be found in Illinois, south-east Wisconsin and the extreme north-west of Indiana.

The **Blue-striped Common Garter Snake** or **Florida Garter Snake** (*Thamnophis sirtalis similis*) is mainly dark brown with a dull yellowish back stripe. Distinctive bright blue side lines, however, run down the body on the 2nd and 3rd scale rows. This sub-species occurs mainly in peninsular Florida.

The **San Francisco Garter Snake** (*Thamnophis sirtalis tetrataenia*) is the rarest and in many people's opinion the most beautiful of all races of Garter Snake. The red marking between the side and back stripes forms a continuous line broken by the light yellow of the back stripe. The top of the head is also light red and the underside of the head is greenish-blue. This sub-species, which is highly endangered, is restricted to San Mateo County in California.

The different races of Common Garter Snake are spread right across America and where they occur are probably the most frequently encountered reptiles, often being seen in the day in moist areas searching for food as they are diurnal in their habits. They can be found in a wide diversity of habitats including meadows, parks, woodland, farms and grassland; from rural even into urban populated areas. Their prey can also vary greatly but frequently includes small amphibians, fish, earthworms, leeches, slugs, molluscs and the occasional young mouse or bird. Anything up to 85 young can be born from one pregnancy after spring matings although far fewer than this is normal (around 20–30). The young, which usually appear around late June to August, can measure up to 23cm in length at birth and take around two to three years to become fully mature.

Other Species

At least six other full species of Garter Snake are recognized, although none of these is likely to become generally available to hobbyists. Their taxonomy is under continual review and most of them at one time or another have been regarded as sub-species of species already described in the text.

Thamnophis angustirostris is recognized as being distinct although it is little known or described as it is known only from specimens collected from Parras, Coahuila, in Mexico.

Thamnophis bovallii was previously regarded as a third sub-species of *Thamnophis marcianus* but is now widely acknowledged as being distinct. It occurs in Nicaragua and Costa Rica.

Thamnophis chrysocephalus is another rarely seen species from Mexico but is more wide-ranging, being recorded from the states of Guerrero, Oaxaca, Puebla and Veracruz.

Thamnophis melanogaster is widely spread across Mexico and probably has at least three sub-species, although its exact taxonomy is under review.

Thamnophis nigronuchalis is also from Mexico and is also under review as to possible sub-species.

Thamnophis sumichrasti, distributed through Mexico and into Central America, has several sub-species that are under review.

As well as these the third sub-species of the Black-necked Garter Snake (*Thamnophis cyrtopsis fulvus*), although stated in this book (page 100) as a sub-species, may now be stated as a full species, *Thamnophis fulvus*.

Glossary

Albino An animal that lacks epidermal pigmentation.

Ambient Term used to express the average level of temperature surrounding an object or animal.

Arboreal Relates to a species which spends most or all of its time in trees or bushes above ground level.

Cloaca A chamber into which the urinary, intestinal and reproductive tract meet.

Colubrid Term relating to any snake species belonging to the colubridae family.

Dimorphic Morphological differences between snakes of the same species, normally relating to visible physical differences between male and female of the same species.

Diurnal Term describing species that are predominantly active during the day.

Ectoparasite A parasite that lives on the exterior of the host animal, such as a tick or mite.

Endemic Confined to a restricted area or region.

Endoparasite A parasite that lives inside the host animal, most commonly a worm.

Exuvial glands Glands that produce a discharge to help loosen the snake's outer skin prior to sloughing.

Family A grouping of related animals falling below an order but above a genus.

Follicle Small anatomical cavity or deep, narrow depression.

Genus A grouping of related animals ranked below a family.

Gestation The period of time during which the young develop inside the mother's body before birth.

Glottis The elongated space between the vocal chords.

Gonad Sex gland which can either be testes in the male or ovaries in the female.

Gravid Term used to describe a female animal if it is carrying eggs or young.

Hemipenes The paired sex organs of a male snake.

Herpetology The study of amphibians and reptiles.

Herptiles Name for any species belonging to *Amphibia* or *Reptilia*.

Husbandry Term used to describe the management of wild animals in captivity.

Hybrid A specimen which is the result of the cross-breeding of two adults of different species.

Inter-grade Term given to a specimen that may be a hybrid of two different species as a result of a natural overlapping in the ranges of the two parent species.

Jacobson's organ The organ in the roof of the mouth used by the snake to taste air and dust particles picked up by the tongue.

Keeled Term used to describe scales that are ridged.

Lateral Relating to the side.

Mandible The lower jaw.

Maxilla The upper jaw.

Necrosis Term for dead skin tissue or an expanding area of dead skin tissue.

Neonates Newly born snakes.

Nominate The first defined description of a species on which variations in sub-species are based.

Nuchal Region at the base of the maxilla (upper skull).

Oesophagus Muscular tube connecting the back of the mouth to the stomach.

Photoperiod The variation in the number of hours of daylight each day throughout the year.

Piscivorous Term used to describe a species which feeds on fish.

Prehensile Adapted for gripping (used mainly to describe the tail in many snakes).

Recurved teeth Teeth which are slightly curved, pointing back into the mouth to assist in the pushing of food into the throat.

Renal Term relating to the kidneys or to the area surrounding them.

Retina Light sensitive membrane at the back of the eye which helps form images which are sent to the brain via the optic nerve.

Sloughing The act by which the snake sheds its outer skin.

Species A distinct subordinate of a genus.

Sub-species A distinct subordinate of a species.

Substrate The substance on which an item rests or lives.

Taxonomy The classification of plant and animal species and groups.

Temperate Term used to describe those regions where the climate is cooler and can also describe the species that inhabit them.

Thermoregulation Act by which a snake regulates its body temperature by moving from areas of warmth to coolness and vice versa.

Tympanum Ear drum.

Vent The anal opening.

Ventral Referring to the under surface of the snake.

Vermiculite A gardening product used widely in reptile husbandry for the artificial incubation of eggs because of its ability to retain water and air.

Vivarium Enclosure used to house herptiles.

Viviparous Applied to species which give birth to live young that have drawn nourishment directly from the parent during development.

Herpetological Societies

The following societies have been established in order to enhance the quality of care in captive snakes as well as other captive reptiles and amphibians.

Europe

British Herpetological Society
c/o Zoological Society of London
Regent's Park
London NW1 4RY
UK

International Herpetological Society
c/o 65 Broadstone Avenue
Walsall
West Midlands WS3 1JA
UK

Association for the Study of Reptiles and Amphibians
c/o Cotswold Wildlife Park
Burford
Oxfordshire OX8 4JW
UK

Dutch Snake Society
c/o Jaag Kooij
Langerveldweg 137
2211 AG Noordwilkerhout
The Netherlands

United States of America

Herpetologists League
c/o Andrew H. Price
Texas Natural Heritage Program
Texas Parks and Wildlife
4200 Smith School Road
Austin TX 78744
USA

Society for the Study of
Amphibians and Reptiles
c/o Dr Douglas Taylor
Department of Zoology
Miami University
Oxford OH 45056
USA

Australia

Australian Affiliation of Herpetological Societies
PO Box R307
Royal Exchange
Sydney
NSW 2000
Australia

Bibliography

Ashton, R. E., and Ashton, P. S. (1981): *Handbook of Reptiles and Amphibians of Florida*, Part One, 'The Snakes'. Windward Publishing Ltd, Florida, USA.

Behler, J. L., and King, F. W. (1979): *The Audubon Society Field Guide to North American Reptiles and Amphibians*. Alfred A. Knopf, New York, USA.

Breene, J. F. (1974): *Encyclopedia of Reptiles and Amphibians*. TFH Publications, Neptune, New Jersey, USA.

Fitch, H. (1965): *An Ecological Study of the Garter Snake Thamnophis sirtalis*. Kansas University Press, Kansas, USA.

Fowler, M. E. (1986): *Zoo and wild animals medicine*. W. B. Saunders Company, Philadelphia, USA.

Frye, F. L. (1981): *Biomedical and Surgical Aspects of Captive Reptile Husbandry*. Krieger Publishing Co Inc, Melbourne, Florida, USA.

Hoff, G. L., Frye, F. L., and Jacobson, E. R. (1984): *Diseases of Amphibians and Reptiles*. Plenum Press, New York, USA.

Mattison, C. (1982): *The Care of Reptiles and Amphibians in Captivity*. Blandford Press, London, UK.

Mattison, C. (1986): *Snakes of the World*. Blandford Press, London, UK.

Mattison, C. (1988): *Keeping and Breeding Snakes*. Blandford Press, London, UK.

Mehrtens, J. M. (1987): *Living Snakes of the World*. Sterling Publishing Co Inc, New York, USA.

Smith, H., and Taylor, E. (1945): *An Annotated Checklist and Key to the Snakes of Mexico*. Smithsonian Institute Press, USA.

Wilson, L. D., and Meyer, J. R. (1985): *The Snakes of Honduras*. Milwaukee Public Museum, USA.

Wright, A. H., and Wright, A. A. (1957): *Handbook of Snakes of the United States and Canada*. Comstock Publishing Associates, New York, USA.

Index

mink, wild 46
mites 68, 75, 76
mongoose 46
motion, caterpillar-type 23, 24
  concertina-type 26
  horizontal-undulatory 24
  snaking 24, 25
Mountain Terrestrial Garter
  Snake 101–2
mouth canker 78
movement 23–7

Narrow-headed Garter Snake 113–14
New Mexico Common Garter
  Snake 118
Northern Chequered Garter
  Snake 105–6
Northern Mexican Garter Snake 104
Northern Ribbon Snake 115
North-western Garter Snake 107–8

oesophagus 17
opossums 47
Oregon Garter Snake 97–8

parasites 68, 75–7
Peninsula Ribbon Snake 115
pet trade, collecting for 45
photoperiod 82
physical injuries 68, 73–5
Pituophis melanoleucus 45
Plains Garter Snake 111–12
predators 44–8
  bird 45
  domestic animal 47–8
  reptile 44–5
  wild mammal 46–7
pregnancy 84
prey 33–4
Puget Sound Common Garter
  Snake 118–19
Pythons 16, 28

quarantine 78

racoons 47
rabbit 47
rat 47
Rattlesnakes 30
rearing 85–7
Red-sided Common Garter Snake 39,
  49, 118
Red-striped Ribbon Snake 110
Red-spotted Common Garter
  Snake 117
reproduction 49–52
reproductive system 18, 20
respiratory diseases 79
Ribbon Snake, Arid Land 110
  Blue-striped 114–15
  Eastern 114
  Gulf Coast 110
  Northern 115

Peninsula 115
  Western 108–11
Roadrunner 45

San Francisco Garter Snake 44, 119
sand eels 64, 85
Santa Cruz Garter Snake 97
scales 20
  head 19
  keeled 20
  upper body 19
  ventral 19, 24
senses 28–32
sexing 80–2
  probes 81
sexual maturity 87
Short-headed Garter Snake 93–4
Sierra Garter Snake 96
sight 28–9
skeleton 14–16
  diagram of 15
skin 20
  problems 68
  sloughing of 21–2
skull 14
skunks 47
sloughing 21–2
  assisting 70–1
  problems of 69–70
slugs 65
smell 28, 30–1
Southern Chequered Garter Snake 106
Southern Black-necked Garter
  Snake 100
species identification key 90–2
steatitis 64, 72
stomartitis 78
swimming 27

tails 80–1
taste 28, 30–1
Tebo-bugs 65, 85
terrestrial snakes 14
Texas Common Garter Snake 117
Thamnophis species 14, 18, 36, 49, 63
Thamnophis angustirostris 120
  bovalli 120
  brachystoma 91, 93–4
  butleri 91, 94–5
  chrysocephalus 120
  couchi 34, 92, 95–8
  couchi aquaticus 96
  couchi atratus 97
  couchi couchi 96
  couchi gigas 97, 98
  couchi hammondi 97
  couchi hydrophilus 97–8
  cyrtopsis 92, 98–100, 103
  cyrtopsis cyrtopsis 99
  cyrtopsis fulvus 100, 120
  cyrtopsis ocellatus 99–100
  elegans 34, 92, 101–3
  elegans biscutatus 102